A Rulebook for Arguments

ANTHONY WESTON

A Rulebook for Arguments

FOURTH EDITION

Hackett Publishing Company, Inc.
Indianapolis/Cambridge

15 14 13 12 11 10   2 3 4 5 6 7

For further information, please address:

Hackett Publishing Company, Inc.
P.O. Box 44937
Indianapolis, IN 46244-0937
www.hackettpublishing.com

Cover image © Tetra Images/Corbis.

Cover design by Jay Hullett
Text design by Abigail Coyle and Anthony Weston
Composition by Agnew's, Inc.
Printed at Victor Graphics, Inc.

Library of Congress Cataloging-in-Publication Data

Weston, Anthony, 1954–
  A rulebook for arguments / Anthony Weston. — 4th edition.
     p. cm.
  ISBN 978-0-87220-954-1 (pbk.)—ISBN 978-0-87220-955-8 (cloth)
  1. Reasoning. 2. Logic. 3. English language—Rhetoric. I. Title.
  BC177.W47 2009
  168—dc22
                                              2008026720

Contents

Preface   ix

Note to the Fourth Edition   x

Introduction   xi

I. Short Arguments: Some General Rules   1

1. Identify premises and conclusion   1
2. Develop your ideas in a natural order   3
3. Start from reliable premises   4
4. Be concrete and concise   5
5. Build on substance, not overtone   5
6. Use consistent terms   6

II. Generalizations   9

7. Use more than one example   10
8. Use representative examples   11
9. Background rates may be crucial   13
10. Statistics need a critical eye   14
11. Consider counterexamples   16

III. Arguments by Analogy   19

12. Analogies require relevantly similar examples   21

IV. Sources   23

13. Cite your sources   24
14. Seek informed sources   24
15. Seek impartial sources   26
16. Cross-check sources   28
17. Use the Web with care   29

V. Arguments about Causes — 31

18. Causal arguments start with correlations — 31
19. Correlations may have alternative explanations — 32
20. Work toward the most likely explanation — 34
21. Expect complexity — 35

VI. Deductive Arguments — 37

22. *Modus ponens* — 38
23. *Modus tollens* — 39
24. Hypothetical syllogism — 40
25. Disjunctive syllogism — 41
26. Dilemma — 42
27. *Reductio ad absurdum* — 43
28. Deductive arguments in several steps — 45

VII. Extended Arguments — 49

29. Explore the issue — 49
30. Spell out basic ideas as arguments — 51
31. Defend basic premises with arguments of their own — 52
32. Consider objections — 54
33. Consider alternatives — 55

VIII. Argumentative Essays — 59

34. Jump right in — 59
35. Make a definite claim or proposal — 60
36. Your argument is your outline — 60
37. Detail objections and meet them — 62
38. Get feedback and use it — 63
39. Modesty, please! — 65

IX. Oral Arguments — 67

40. Reach out to your audience — 67
41. Be fully present — 68
42. Signpost your argument — 69
43. Offer something positive — 70
44. Use visual aids sparingly — 71
45. End in style — 72

Appendix I: Some Common Fallacies   73

Appendix II: Definitions   81

D1. When terms are unclear, get specific   81
D2. When terms are contested, work from the
    clear cases   83
D3. Definitions don't replace arguments   85

Resources   87

Preface

This book is a brief introduction to the art of making arguments. It sticks to the bare essentials. I have found that students and writers often need just such a list of reminders and rules, not lengthy introductory explanations. This book is therefore organized around specific rules, illustrated and explained soundly but above all briefly. It is not a textbook but a *rule*book.

Instructors too, I have found, often wish to assign such a rulebook, a treatment that students can consult and understand on their own and that therefore does not claim too much class time. Here again, it is important to be brief—the point is to help students get on with their actual arguments—but the rules must be stated with enough substance that an instructor can simply refer a student to Rule 6 or Rule 16 rather than give an entire explanation each time it is needed. Brief but self-sufficient— that is the fine line I have tried to follow.

This rulebook also can be used in a course that gives critical attention to arguments. It will need to be supplemented with exercises and more examples, but many texts are already available that consist largely or wholly of such exercises and examples. *Those* texts, however, also need to be supplemented—with what this rulebook offers: simple rules for putting good arguments together. We do not want our students to come out of critical thinking courses knowing only how to shoot down (or just *at*) selected fallacies. Critical thinking can be practiced in a far more constructive spirit. This book is one attempt to suggest how.

Note to the Fourth Edition

Logic doesn't change, but the times do. Today students are coming to college better prepared, and high schools and even middle schools are teaching critical thinking themselves. A rulebook of this sort, still very introductory, can ask more and go further than it did when I first wrote it twenty years ago.

This new edition therefore has been significantly overhauled. Three chapters on argumentative essays have been replaced by one chapter on extended arguments generally, one on argumentative essays proper, and a new chapter on oral arguments. Chapter V, on causal arguments, has a sharper and more practical focus. There is more on the use of numbers and a new section on Web sources, while a few themes that previously had a section of their own have been blended with others or have migrated to the appendixes. You'll also notice that the numbering of the rules is simplified: the rules are now numbered consecutively, from 1 to 45.

My warmest thanks once again go to so many colleagues, friends, and students for their support and encouragement. For especially close readings and much helpful feedback in the preparation of this fourth edition, special acknowledgment is due to three long-time users of this book: Ann Cahill, my colleague at Elon University; Charles Kay of Wofford College; and Debra Nails of Michigan State University. My gratitude also to Deborah Wilkes at Hackett Publishing Company for her deft oversight of the whole process, and to my partner Amy Halberstadt for showing me how the chapter on causal arguments could be so much more constructively framed. Criticisms and suggestions, as always, are welcome.

Anthony Weston
Spring 2008

Introduction

What's the point of arguing?

Many people think that arguing is simply stating their prejudices in a new form. This is why many people also think that arguments are unpleasant and pointless. One dictionary definition for "argument" is "disputation." In this sense we sometimes say that two people "*have* an argument": a verbal fistfight. It happens often enough. But it is not what arguments really are.

In this book, "to give an argument" means to offer a set of reasons or evidence in support of a conclusion. Here an argument is not simply a statement of certain views, and it is not simply a dispute. Arguments are efforts to *support* certain views with reasons. Arguments in this sense are not pointless; in fact, they are essential.

Argument is essential, in the first place, because it is a way of finding out which views are better than others. Not all views are equal. Some conclusions can be supported by good reasons. Others have much weaker support. But often we don't know which are which. We need to give arguments for different conclusions and then assess those arguments to see how strong they really are.

Here argument is a means of *inquiry*. Some philosophers and activists have argued, for instance, that the factory farming of animals for meat causes immense suffering to animals and is therefore unjustified and immoral. Are they right? We can't necessarily tell just by consulting our current opinions. Many issues are involved—we need to examine the arguments. Do we have moral obligations to other species, for instance, or is only human suffering really bad? How well can humans live without meat? Some vegetarians have lived to very old ages. Does this show that vegetarian diets are healthier? Or is it irrelevant when you consider that some nonvegetarians also have lived to very old ages? (You might make some progress by asking whether vegetarians live to old age at a higher *rate.*) Or might healthier people tend to become vegetarians, rather than vice versa? All of these questions need to be considered carefully, and the answers are not clear in advance.

Argument is essential for another reason too. Once we have arrived at a conclusion that is well supported by reasons, we use arguments to explain and defend it. A good argument doesn't merely repeat conclusions. Instead it offers reasons and evidence so that other people can make up their minds for themselves. If you become convinced that we should indeed change the way we raise and use animals, for example, you must use arguments to explain how you arrived at your conclusion. That is how you will convince others: by offering the reasons and evidence that convinced *you.* It is not a mistake to have strong views. The mistake is to have nothing else.

Argument grows on you

Typically we learn to "argue" by *assertion.* That is, we tend to start with our conclusions—our desires or opinions—without a whole lot to back them up. And it works, sometimes, at least when we're very young. What could be better?

Real argument, by contrast, takes time and practice. Marshaling our reasons, proportioning our conclusions to the actual evidence, considering objections, and all the rest—these are acquired skills. We have to grow up a little. We have to put aside our desires and our opinions for a while and actually *think.*

School may help—or not. In courses concerned with teaching ever-larger sets of facts or techniques, students are seldom encouraged to ask the sorts of questions that arguments answer. Sure, our Constitution mandates the Electoral College—that's a fact—but is it still a good idea? (For that matter, was it ever a good idea? What were the reasons for it, anyway?) Sure, many scientists believe that there is life elsewhere in the universe, but why? What's the argument? Reasons can be given for different answers. In the end, ideally, you will not only learn some of those reasons but also learn how to weigh them up—and how to seek out more yourself.

Mostly, again, it takes time and practice. This book can help! Moreover, the practice of argument turns out to have some attractions of its own. Our minds become more flexible, open-ended, and alert. We come to appreciate how much difference our own critical thinking can really make. From everyday family life to politics, science, philosophy, and even religion, arguments are constantly offered to us for our consideration, and we may in turn offer back our own. Think of argument as a way to make your own place within these unfolding, ongoing dialogues. What could be better than *that?*

Outline of this book

This book begins by discussing fairly simple arguments and moves to extended arguments and their use in essays and oral presentations at the end.

Chapters I–VI are about composing and assessing *short* arguments. Short arguments simply offer their reasons and evidence briefly, usually in a few sentences or a paragraph. We begin with short arguments for several reasons. First, they are common: in fact so common that they are part of every day's conversation. Second, longer arguments are usually elaborations of short arguments, or a series of short arguments linked together. If you learn to write and assess short arguments first, then you can extend your skills to longer arguments in essays or presentations.

A third reason for beginning with short arguments is that they are the best illustrations both of the common argument forms and of the typical mistakes in arguments. In longer arguments, it can be harder to pick out the main points—and the main problems. Therefore, although some of the rules may seem obvious when first stated, remember that you have the benefit of a simple example. Other rules are hard enough to appreciate even in short arguments.

Chapter VII guides you into sketching and then elaborating an extended argument, considering objections and alternatives as you do. Chapter VIII guides you from there into writing an argumentative essay. Chapter IX then adds rules specifically about oral presentation. Again, all of these chapters depend on Chapters I–VI, since extended arguments like these essentially combine and elaborate the kinds of short arguments that Chapters I–VI discuss. Don't skip ahead to the later chapters, then, even if you come to this book primarily for help writing an essay or doing a presentation. The book is short enough that you can read it through from the beginning; if you do, when you arrive at those later chapters you will have the tools you need to use them well. Instructors might wish to assign Chapters I–VI early in the term and Chapters VII–IX when the time comes for essays and presentations.

Two appendixes close out the book. The first is a listing of fallacies: types of misleading arguments that are so tempting and common, they even have their own names. The second offers three rules for constructing and evaluating definitions. Use them when you need them!

I

Short Arguments:
Some General Rules

Arguments begin by marshaling reasons and organizing them in a clear and fair way. Chapter I offers general rules for composing short arguments. Chapters II–VI discuss specific *kinds* of short arguments.

Identify premises and conclusion

The very first step in making an argument is to ask yourself what you are trying to prove. What is your conclusion? Remember that the conclusion is the statement for which you are giving reasons. The statements that give your reasons are your *premises.*

Consider these lines from Winston Churchill:

I am an optimist. It does not seem to be much use being anything else.

This is an argument—not just an amusing quip—because Churchill is giving a *reason* to be an optimist: his premise is that "It does not seem to be much use being anything else."

Premises and conclusion are not always so obvious. Sherlock Holmes has to explain one of his deductions in "The Adventure of Silver Blaze":

A dog was kept in the stables, and yet, though someone had been in and had fetched out a horse, [the dog] had not barked. . . . Obviously the . . . visitor was someone whom the dog knew well.[1]

Holmes has two premises. One is explicit: the dog did not bark at the visitor. The other is a general fact that Holmes assumes we know about dogs: dogs bark at strangers. Together these premises imply that the visitor was not a stranger. It turns out that this is the key to solving the mystery.

When you are using arguments as a means of inquiry, you sometimes may start with no more than the conclusion you wish to defend. State it clearly, first of all. Maybe you want to take Churchill a step further and argue that you and I should be optimists too. If so, say so explicitly. Then ask yourself what reasons you have for drawing that conclusion. What reasons can you give to prove that we should be optimists?

You could appeal to Churchill's authority. If Churchill recommends optimism, who are you or I to quibble? This appeal will not get you very far, however, since equally famous people have recommended pessimism. You need to think about the question on your own. Again, what is *your* reason for thinking that we should be optimists?

One reason could be that optimism boosts your energy to work for success, whereas if you feel defeated in advance you may never even try. Optimists are more likely to succeed, to achieve their goals. (Maybe this is what Churchill meant as well.) If this is your premise, say so explicitly.

This book offers you a ready list of different forms that arguments can take. Use this list to develop your premises. To defend a generalization, for instance, check Chapter II. It will remind you that you need to give a series of examples as premises, and it will tell you what sorts of examples to look for. If your conclusion requires a deductive argument like those explained in Chapter VI, the rules outlined in that chapter will tell you what types of premises you need. You may have to try several different arguments before you find one that works well.

---

[1] Sir Arthur Conan Doyle, "The Adventure of Silver Blaze," in *The Complete Sherlock Holmes* (Garden City, NY: Garden City Books, 1930), p. 199.

Develop your ideas in a natural order

Short arguments are usually developed in one or two paragraphs. Put the conclusion first, followed by your reasons, or set out your premises first and draw the conclusion at the end. In any case, set out your ideas in an order that unfolds your line of thought most clearly for the reader.

Consider this short argument by Bertrand Russell:

> The evils of the world are due to moral defects quite as much as to lack of intelligence. But the human race has not hitherto discovered any method of eradicating moral defects. . . . Intelligence, on the contrary, is easily improved by methods known to every competent educator. Therefore, until some method of teaching virtue has been discovered, progress will have to be sought by improvement of intelligence rather than of morals.[2]

Each sentence in this passage prepares the way for the next one, and then the next one steps smoothly up to bat. Russell begins by pointing out the two sources of evil in the world: "moral defects," as he puts it, and lack of intelligence. He then claims that we do not know how to correct "moral defects," but that we do know how to correct lack of intelligence. Therefore—notice that the word "therefore" clearly marks his conclusion —progress will have to come by improving intelligence.

Getting an argument to unfold in this smooth sort of way is a real accomplishment. It's not easy to find just the right place for each part—and plenty of wrong places are available. Suppose Russell instead argued like this:

> The evils of the world are due to moral defects quite as much as to lack of intelligence. Until some method of teaching virtue has been discovered, progress will have to be sought by improvement of intelligence rather than of morals. Intelligence is easily improved by methods known to every competent educator. The human race has not hitherto discovered any means of eradicating moral defects.

---

[2] Bertrand Russell, *Skeptical Essays* (1935; reprint, London: Allen & Unwin, 1977), p. 127.

These are the same premises and conclusion, but they are in a different order, and the word "therefore" has been omitted before the conclusion. Now the argument is much harder to understand, and therefore also much less persuasive. The premises do not fit together naturally, and you have to read the passage twice just to figure out what the conclusion is. Don't count on your readers to be so patient.

Expect to rearrange your argument several times to find the most natural order. The rules discussed in this book should help. You can use them to figure out not only what kinds of premises you need but also how to arrange them in the best order.

Start from reliable premises

No matter how well you argue from premises to conclusion, your conclusion will be weak if your premises are weak.

> Nobody in the world today is really happy. Therefore, it seems that human beings are just not made for happiness. Why should we expect what we can never find?

The premise of this argument is the statement that nobody in the world today is really happy. Sometimes, on certain rainy afternoons or in certain moods, this may almost seem true. But ask yourself if this premise really is plausible. Is *nobody* in the world today really happy? Ever? At the very least, this premise needs some serious defense, and very likely it is just not true. This argument cannot show, then, that human beings are not made for happiness or that you or I should not expect to be happy.

Sometimes it is easy to start from reliable premises. You may have well-known examples at hand or reliable sources that are clearly in agreement. Other times it is harder. If you are not sure about the reliability of a premise, you may need to do some research and/or give an argument for the premise itself (see Rule 31 for more on this point). If you find you *cannot* argue adequately for your premise(s), then, of course, you need to try some other premise!

Be concrete and concise

Avoid abstract, vague, and general terms. "We hiked for hours in the sun" is a hundred times better than "It was an extended period of laborious exertion." Be concise too. Airy elaboration just loses everyone in a fog of words.

NO:

> For those whose roles primarily involved the performance of services, as distinguished from assumption of leadership responsibilities, the main pattern seems to have been a response to the leadership's invoking obligations that were concomitants of the status of membership in the societal community and various of its segmental units. The closest modern analogy is the military service performed by an ordinary citizen, except that the leader of the Egyptian bureaucracy did not need a special emergency to invoke legitimate obligations.[3]

YES:

> In ancient Egypt the common people were liable to be conscripted for work.

Build on substance, not overtone

Offer actual reasons; don't just play on the overtones of words.

NO:

> Having so disgracefully allowed her once-proud passenger railroads to fade into obscurity, America is honor bound to restore them now!

This is supposed to be an argument for restoring (more) passenger rail service. But it offers no evidence for this conclusion whatsoever, just

---

[3] Talcott Parsons, *Societies: Evolutionary and Comparative Perspectives* (Englewood Cliffs, NJ: Prentice Hall, 1966), p. 56. I owe the quotation and the rewritten version that follows to Stanislas Andreski, *Social Sciences as Sorcery* (New York: St. Martin's Press, 1972), Chapter 6.

some emotionally loaded words—shopworn words, too, like a politician on automatic. Did passenger rail "fade" because of something "America" did or didn't do? What was "disgraceful" about this? Many "once-proud" institutions outlive their times, after all—we're not obliged to restore them all. What does it mean to say America is "honor bound" to do this? Have promises been made and broken? By whom?

Much can be said for restoring passenger rail, especially in this era when the ecological and economic costs of highways are becoming enormous. The problem is that this argument does not say it. It lets the emotional charge of the words do all the work, and therefore really does no work at all. We're left exactly where we started. Overtones may sometimes persuade even when they shouldn't, of course—but remember, here we are looking for actual, concrete evidence.

Likewise, do not try to make your argument look good by using emotionally loaded words to label the other side. Generally, people advocate a position for serious and sincere reasons. Try to figure out their view—try to understand their *reasons*—even if you disagree entirely. For example, people who question a new technology are probably not in favor of "going back to the caves." (What *are* they in favor of? Maybe you need to ask.) Likewise, a person who believes in evolution is not claiming that her grandparents were monkeys. (And again: what *does* she think?) In general, if you can't imagine how anyone could hold the view you are attacking, you probably just don't understand it yet.

Use consistent terms

Short arguments normally have a single theme or thread. They carry one idea through several steps. Therefore, couch that idea in clear and carefully chosen terms, and mark each new step by using those very same terms again.

NO:

When you learn about other cultures, you start to realize the variety of human customs. This new understanding of the diversity of social practices may give you a new appreciation of other ways of life. Therefore, studying anthropology tends to make you more tolerant.

YES:

When you learn about other cultures, you start to realize the variety of human customs. When you start to realize the variety of human customs, you tend to become more tolerant. Therefore, when you learn about other cultures, you tend to become more tolerant.

The "Yes" version might not be stylish, but it *is* crystal clear, whereas the "No" version hardly seems like the same argument. One simple feature makes the difference: the "Yes" argument repeats its key terms, while the "No" version uses a new phrase for each key idea every time the idea recurs. For example, "learning about other cultures" is redescribed in the "No" version's conclusion as "studying anthropology." The result is that the connection between premises and conclusion is lost in the underbrush. It's interesting underbrush, maybe, but you are still liable to get stuck in it.

Re-using the same key phrases can feel repetitive, of course, so you may be tempted to reach for your thesaurus. Don't go there! The logic depends on clear connections between premises and between premises and conclusion. It remains essential to use a consistent term for each idea. If you are concerned about style—as sometimes you should be, of course—then go for the tightest argument, not the most flowery.

MOST CONCISE:

When you learn about other cultures, you start to realize the variety of human customs, a realization that in turn tends to make you more tolerant.

You can talk about studying anthropology and the like, if you wish, as you explain each step in turn.

II

Generalizations

Some arguments offer one or more examples in support of a generalization.

> Women in earlier times were married very young. Juliet in Shakespeare's *Romeo and Juliet* was not even fourteen years old. In the Middle Ages, thirteen was the normal age of marriage for a Jewish woman. And during the Roman Empire, many Roman women were married at age thirteen or younger.

This argument generalizes from three examples—Juliet, Jewish women in the Middle Ages, and Roman women during the Roman Empire—to "many" or *most* women in earlier times. To show the form of this argument most clearly, we can list the premises separately, with the conclusion on the "bottom line":

> Juliet in Shakespeare's play was not even fourteen years old.
>
> Jewish women during the Middle Ages were normally married at thirteen.
>
> Many Roman women during the Roman Empire were married at age thirteen or younger.
>
> Therefore, women in earlier times were married very young.

It is helpful to write short arguments in this way when we need to see exactly how they work.

When do premises like these adequately support a generalization?

One requirement, of course, is that the examples be accurate. Remember Rule 3: start from reliable premises! If Juliet *wasn't* around fourteen, or if most Roman or Jewish women *weren't* married at thirteen or younger, then the argument is much weaker. If none of the premises can be supported, there is no argument at all. To check an argument's examples, or to find good examples for your own arguments, you may need to do some research.

But suppose the examples *are* accurate. Even then, generalizing from them is a tricky business. The rules in this chapter offer a short checklist for assessing arguments by example.

7

Use more than one example

A single example can sometimes be used for the sake of *illustration*. The example of Juliet alone might illustrate early marriage. But a single example offers next to no *support* for a generalization. Juliet alone may just be an exception. One spectacularly miserable billionaire does not prove that rich people in general are unhappy. More than one example is needed.

NO:

French fries are unhealthy (high in fat).

Therefore, all fast foods are unhealthy.

YES:

French fries are unhealthy (high in fat).

Milkshakes are unhealthy (high in fat and sugar).

Deep-fried chicken and cheeseburgers are unhealthy (high in fat).

Therefore, all fast foods are unhealthy.

The "Yes" version may still be weak (Rule 11 returns to it), but it certainly gives you much more to chew on, so to speak, than the "No" version.

In a generalization about a small set of things, the strongest argument should consider all, or at least many, of the examples. A generalization about your siblings should consider each of them in turn, for instance, and a generalization about all the planets in the solar system can do the same.

Generalizations about larger sets of things require picking out a *sample*. We certainly cannot list all women in earlier times who married young. Instead, our argument must offer a few women as examples of the rest. How many examples are required depends partly on how representative they are, a point the next rule takes up. It also depends partly on the size of the set being generalized about. Large sets usually require more examples. The claim that your town is full of remarkable people requires more evidence than the claim that, say, your friends are remarkable people. Depending on how many friends you have, even just two or three examples might be enough to establish that your friends are remarkable people; but, unless your town is tiny, many more examples are required to show that your town is full of remarkable people.

8. Use representative examples

Even a large number of examples may still misrepresent the set being generalized about. A large number of examples of ancient Roman women, for instance, might establish very little about women generally, since ancient Roman women are not necessarily representative of other women. The argument needs to consider women from other early times and from other parts of the world as well.

> Everyone in my neighborhood favors McGraw for president. Therefore, McGraw is sure to win.

This argument is weak because single neighborhoods seldom represent the voting population as a whole. A well-to-do neighborhood may favor a candidate who is unpopular with everyone else. Student wards in university towns regularly are carried by candidates who do poorly elsewhere. Besides, we seldom have good evidence even about neighborhood views. The set of people eager to display their political preferences to the world is probably not a representative cross-section of the neighborhood as a whole.

A *good* argument that "McGraw is sure to win" requires a representative sample of the entire voting population. It is not easy to construct such a sample. Public opinion polls, for instance, construct their samples very carefully. They learned the hard way. The classic example is a 1936 poll conducted by the *Literary Digest* to predict the outcome of the presidential contest between Roosevelt and Landon. Names were taken, as they are now, from telephone listings, and also from automobile registration lists. The number of people polled was certainly not too small: more than two million "ballots" were counted. The poll predicted a wide victory for Landon. In the event, though, Roosevelt won easily. In retrospect it is easy to see what went wrong. In 1936, only a select portion of the population owned telephones and cars. The sample was sharply biased toward wealthy and urban voters, more of whom supported Landon.

Polls have improved since then. Nonetheless, there are still worries about the representativeness of their samples, and they still regularly forecast elections wrong. For example, these days most of my students don't have landlines at all—only cell phones with unlisted numbers. The pollsters aren't calling *them*. Phone polls may actually be getting less representative again.

It is often an open question, then, just how representative a given sample may be. Anticipate this danger! Do some research. Juliet, for example, is just one woman. Is she representative of women in her time and place? In Shakespeare's play, Juliet's mother says to her:

> Think of marriage now; younger than you,
> Here in Verona, ladies of esteem,
> Are made already mothers. By my count,
> I was your mother much upon these years
> That you are now a maid . . .
>
> (1.3.69–73)

This passage suggests that Juliet's marriage at fourteen is not exceptional; in fact, fourteen seems to be a little on the old side.

In general, look for the most accurate cross-section you can find of the population being generalized about. If you want to know what students think about some subject at your university, don't just ask the people you know or generalize from what you hear in class. Unless you know quite a range of people and take quite a range of classes, your personal "sample" is not likely to mirror the whole student body. Similarly, if you want to know what people in other countries think about the United States, don't just ask foreign tourists—for of course they are the ones who chose to come here. A careful look at a range of foreign media should give you a more representative picture.

Background rates may be crucial

To persuade you that I am a first-rate archer, it is not enough to show you a bull's-eye I have made. You should ask (politely, to be sure), "Yes, but how many times did you *miss?*" Getting a bull's-eye in one shot tells quite a different story than getting a bull's-eye in, say, a thousand, even though in both cases I genuinely do have a bull's-eye to my name. You need a little more data.

Or again:

> Leon's horoscope told him that he would meet a vivacious new stranger, and lo and behold he did! Therefore, horoscopes are reliable.

Dramatic as such an example may be, the problem is that we are only looking at one case in which a horoscope came true. To properly evaluate this evidence, we need to know something else as well: how many horoscopes *didn't* come true. When I survey my classes, we can usually find a few Leons out of twenty or thirty students. The other nineteen or twenty-nine horoscopes go nowhere. But a kind of prediction that comes true only once out of twenty or thirty tries is hardly reliable—it's just lucky once in a while. It may have some dramatic successes, like my archery, but its success *rate* may still be abysmal.

To evaluate the reliability of any argument featuring a few vivid examples, then, we need to know the ratio between the number of "hits," so to speak, and the number of *tries*. It's a question of representativeness again. Are the featured examples the only ones there are? Is the rate impressively high or low?

Another case in point:

The "Bermuda Triangle" area off Bermuda is famous as a place where many ships and planes have mysteriously disappeared. Avoid it at all costs! There have been several dozen disappearances in the past decade alone.

No doubt. But several dozen out of how many ships and planes that *passed through* the area? Several dozen, or several hundred thousand? If only twenty, say, have disappeared out of maybe two hundred thousand, then the disappearance *rate* in the Bermuda Triangle may well be normal, or even unusually low—certainly not mysterious.

Statistics need a critical eye

Some people see numbers—*any* numbers—in an argument and conclude from that fact alone that it must be a good argument. Statistics seem to have an aura of authority and definiteness (and did you know that 88 percent of doctors agree?). In fact, though, numbers take as much critical thinking as any other kind of evidence. Don't turn off your brain!

> After an era when some athletic powerhouse universities were accused of exploiting student athletes, leaving them to flunk out once their eligibility expired, college athletes are now graduating at higher rates. Many schools are now graduating more than 50 percent of their athletes.

Fifty percent, eh? Pretty impressive! But this figure, at first so persuasive, does not really do the job it claims to do.

First, although "many" schools graduate more than 50 percent of their athletes, it appears that some do not—so this figure may well exclude the most exploitative schools that really concerned people in the first place.

The argument does offer graduation rates. But it would be useful to know how a "more than 50 percent" graduation rate compares with the graduation rate for *all* students at the same institutions. If it is significantly lower, athletes may still be getting the shaft.

Most importantly, this argument offers no reason to believe that college athletes' graduation rates are actually *improving,* because no comparison to any previous rate is offered! The conclusion claims that the graduation rate is now "higher," but without knowing the previous rates it is impossible to tell.

Numbers may offer incomplete evidence in other ways too. Rule 9, for example, tells us that knowing background rates may be crucial. Correspondingly, when an argument offers rates or percentages, the relevant background information usually must include the *number* of examples. Car thefts on campus may have doubled, but if this means that two cars were stolen rather than one, there's not much to worry about.

Another statistical pitfall is *over-precision:*

> Every year this campus wastes 412,067 paper and plastic cups. It's time to switch to reusable cups!

I'm all for ending waste too, and I'm sure the amount of campus waste is huge. But no one really knows the precise number of cups wasted—and it's extremely unlikely to be exactly the same every year. Here the appearance of exactness makes the evidence seem more authoritative than it really is.

Be wary, also, of numbers that are easily manipulated. Pollsters know very well that the way a question is asked can shape how it is answered. These days we are even seeing "polls" that try to change people's minds about, say, a political candidate, just by asking loaded questions ("If you were to discover that she is a liar and a cheat, how would that change your vote?"). Then too, many apparently "hard" statistics are actually based on guesswork or extrapolation, such as data about semi-legal or illegal activities. Since people have a major motive not to reveal or report things like drug use, under-the-counter transactions, hiring illegal aliens, and the like, beware of any confident generalizations about how widespread they are.

Yet again:

> If kids keep watching more TV at current rates, by 2025 they'll have no time left to sleep!

Right, and by 2040 they'll be watching thirty-six hours a day. Extrapolation in such cases is perfectly possible mathematically, but after a certain point it tells you nothing.

Consider counterexamples

Counterexamples are examples that contradict your generalization. No fun—maybe. But counterexamples actually can be a generalizer's best friends, if you use them early and use them well. Look for them on purpose and systematically. It is the best way to sharpen your own generalizations and to probe more deeply into your theme.

Consider this argument once again:

> French fries are unhealthy (high in fat).
>
> Milkshakes are unhealthy (high in fat and sugar).
>
> Deep-fried chicken and cheeseburgers are unhealthy (high in fat).
>
> Therefore, all fast foods are unhealthy.

This argument offers multiple and apparently representative examples. However, as soon as you start thinking about counterexamples instead of just more examples, you will find that the argument overgeneralizes. Subway sandwiches, for example, are "fast food" as well, but vegetables and buns are the primary ingredients, meats and cheeses are add-ons, and nothing is deep-fried. So it turns out that not *all* fast foods are unhealthy.

If you can think of counterexamples to a generalization that you want to defend, then you need to adjust your generalization. If the last argument were yours, for instance, you might change the conclusion to "*Many* fast foods are unhealthy."

Such a counterexample may also prompt you to think more deeply about what it *is* about fast foods that tends to make them unhealthy. Is it partly that deep-frying—with the huge fat load that results—is such a quick and easy way of cooking? Highly processed foods, such as fast-food meat and cheese and milkshake ingredients, also tend to be fattier or unhealthy in other ways. So maybe what you really want to say is that the demand for quick cooking and cheap, standardized ingredients tends to make the results less healthy (although this is not invariable, as the example of subway sandwiches suggests). This is a more subtle and interesting claim than the original one, and gives your thinking more room to move.

Ask yourself about counterexamples when you are assessing others' arguments as well as evaluating your own. Ask whether *their* conclusions might have to be revised and limited, or rethought in more subtle and complex directions. The same rules apply both to others' arguments and to yours. The only difference is that you have a chance to correct your overgeneralizations yourself.

III

Arguments by Analogy

There is an exception to Rule 7 ("Use more than one example"). *Arguments by analogy*, rather than multiplying examples to support a generalization, argue from *one* specific example to another, reasoning that because the two examples are alike in many ways, they are also alike in one further specific way.

For example, here is how a doctor argues that everyone should have a regular physical checkup:

> People take in their car for servicing and checkups every few months without complaint. Why shouldn't they take similar care of their bodies?[4]

This argument suggests that getting a regular physical checkup is *like* taking your car in for regular servicing. Cars need that kind of attention—otherwise, major problems may develop. Aren't our bodies like that too?

> People should take their cars in for regular service and checkups (otherwise major problems may develop).
>
> People's bodies are *like* cars (because human bodies, too, are complex systems that can develop problems if not regularly checked up).
>
> Therefore, people should take themselves in for regular "service" and checkups too.

---

[4] Dr. John Beary III, quoted in "News You Can Use," *U.S. News and World Report,* 11 August 1986, p. 61.

Notice the italicized word "like" in the second premise. When an argument stresses the likeness between two cases, it is very probably an argument from analogy.

Here is another striking example.

> An interesting switch was pulled in Rome yesterday by Adam Nordwell, an American Chippewa chief. As he descended his plane from California dressed in full tribal regalia, Nordwell announced in the name of the American Indian people that he was taking possession of Italy "by right of discovery" in the same way that Christopher Columbus did in America. "I proclaim this day the day of the discovery of Italy," said Nordwell. "What right did Columbus have to discover America when it had already been inhabited for thousands of years? The same right I now have to come to Italy and proclaim the discovery of your country."[5]

Nordwell is suggesting that his "discovery" of Italy is *like* Columbus's "discovery" of America in at least one important way: both Nordwell and Columbus claimed a country that already had been inhabited by its own people for centuries. Thus, Nordwell insists that he has as much "right" to claim Italy as Columbus had to claim America. But, of course, Nordwell has no right at all to claim Italy. It follows that Columbus had no right at all to claim America.

> Nordwell has no right to claim Italy for another people, let alone "by right of discovery" (because Italy has been inhabited by its own people for centuries).

> Columbus's claim to America "by right of discovery" is *like* Nordwell's claim to Italy (America, too, had been inhabited by its own people for centuries).

> Therefore, Columbus had no right to claim America for another people, let alone "by right of discovery."

How do we evaluate arguments by analogy?

The first premise of an argument by analogy makes a claim about the example used as an analogy. Remember Rule 3: make sure this premise

---

[5] *Miami News,* 23 September 1973.

is true. It's true that cars need regular service and checkups to keep major problems from developing, for instance, and it's true that Adam Nordwell could not claim Italy for the Chippewa.

The second premise in arguments by analogy claims that the example in the first premise is *like* the example about which the argument draws a conclusion. Evaluating this premise is harder and needs a rule of its own.

Analogies require relevantly similar examples

Arguments by analogy do not require that the example used as an analogy be *exactly* like the example in the conclusion. Our bodies are not just like cars, after all. We are flesh and bone, not metal; we don't have wheels or seats or windshield wipers. Analogies require *relevant* similarities. What cars are made of or exactly what their parts are is irrelevant to the doctor's point. The argument is about the upkeep of complex systems.

One relevant difference between our bodies and our cars is that our bodies do not need regular "service" in the way our cars do. Cars regularly need oil changes, new pumps or transmissions, and the like. But replacing body parts or fluids is much rarer: think organ transplants or blood transfusions. On the other hand, it's true that we need regular checkups—otherwise, problems can develop undetected—and older and strenuously used bodies, like older and higher mileage cars, may need checkups more often. So the doctor's analogy is partly successful. The "service" part is somewhat weak, in my view, but the checkup part is persuasive.

Likewise, twentieth-century Italy is not just like fifteenth-century America. Italy is known to every twentieth-century schoolchild, whereas America was unknown to much of the world in the fifteenth century. Nordwell is not an explorer, and a commercial jet is not the *Santa Maria*. But these differences are not relevant to Nordwell's analogy. Nordwell simply means to remind us that it is senseless to claim a country already inhabited by its own people. Whether that land is known to the world's schoolchildren, or how the "discoverer" arrived there, is not important. The more appropriate reaction might have been to try to establish diplomatic relations, as we would try to do today if somehow the land and people of Italy had just been discovered. *That's* Nordwell's point, and, taken in that way, his analogy makes a good (and unsettling) argument.

One famous argument uses an analogy to try to establish the existence of a Creator of the world. We can infer the existence of a Creator from the order and beauty of the world, this argument claims, just as we can infer the existence of an architect or carpenter when we see a beautiful and well-built house. Spelled out in premise-and-conclusion form:

> Beautiful and well-built houses must have "makers": designers and builders.
>
> The world is *like* a beautiful and well-built house.
>
> Therefore, the world also must have a "maker": a Designer and Builder, God.

Again, more examples are not necessarily needed here. The argument turns on the similarity of the world to *one* well-understood example, a house.

Whether the world really *is* relevantly similar to a house, though, is not so clear. We know quite a bit about the causes of houses. But houses are *parts* of the world. We know very little, actually, about the structure of the world (the universe) as a *whole* or about what sorts of causes it might be expected to have. The philosopher David Hume discussed this argument in his *Dialogues Concerning Natural Religion* and asked:

> Is part of nature a rule for the whole? . . . Think [of how] wide a step you have taken when you compared houses . . . to the universe, and from their similarity in some circumstances inferred a similarity in their causes. . . . Does not the great disproportion bar all comparison and inference?[6]

Hume therefore suggests that the universe is *not* relevantly similar to a house. Houses indeed imply "makers" beyond themselves, but for all we know the universe as a whole may contain its cause within itself, or perhaps has some kind of cause unique to universes. This analogy, then, makes a poor argument. Some other kind of argument is probably needed if the existence of God is to be inferred from the nature of the world.

---

[6] David Hume, *Dialogues Concerning Natural Religion* (1779; reprint, Indianapolis: Hackett Publishing Company, 1980), p. 19.

IV

Sources

No one can be an expert through direct experience on everything there is to know. We do not live in ancient times ourselves and therefore cannot know first-hand at what age women tended to marry back then. Few of us have enough experience to judge which kinds of cars are safest in a crash. We do not know first-hand what is really happening in Sri Lanka or the state legislature, or even in the average American classroom or street corner. Instead, we must rely on others—better-situated people, organizations, surveys, or reference works—to tell us much of what we need to know about the world. We argue like this:

> X (a source that ought to know) says that Y.
>
> Therefore, Y is true.

For instance:

> Carl Sagan says that there could be life on Mars.
>
> Therefore, there could be life on Mars.

It's a risky business, though. Supposedly expert sources may be over-confident, or may be misled, or may not even be reliable. And everyone has biases, after all, even if innocent ones. Once again we must consider a checklist of standards that truly authoritative sources need to meet.

Cite your sources

Some factual assertions, of course, are so obvious or well known that they do not need support at all. It is usually not necessary to *prove* that the United States has fifty states or that Juliet loved Romeo. However, a precise figure for the current population of the United States does need a citation. Likewise, the claim that Juliet was only fourteen should cite a few Shakespearean lines in support.

NO:

> I once read that there are cultures in which makeup and clothes are mostly men's business, not women's.

If you're arguing about whether men and women everywhere follow the gender roles familiar to us, this is a relevant example—a striking case of different gender roles. But few of us know anything about this sort of difference first-hand. To nail down the argument, you need to call upon a fully cited source.

YES:

> Carol Beckwith, in "Niger's Wodaabe" (*National Geographic* 164, no. 4 [October 1983], pp. 483–509), reports that among the West African Fulani peoples such as the Wodaabe, makeup and clothes are mostly men's business.

Citation styles vary—you may need a handbook of style to find the appropriate style for your purposes—but all include the same basic information: enough so that others can easily find the source on their own.

Seek informed sources

Sources must be qualified to make the statements they make. Honda mechanics are qualified to discuss the merits of different Hondas, midwives and obstetricians are qualified to discuss pregnancy and childbirth, teachers are qualified to discuss the state of their schools, and so on. These sources are qualified because they have the appropriate background and information. For the best information about global climate change, go to climatologists, not politicians.

Where a source's qualifications are not immediately clear, an argument must explain them briefly. Carl Sagan says that there could be life on Mars, eh? But who is Carl Sagan? Here is the answer: Sagan was an astronomer and astrobiologist, a leader in the space program, and among the designers of the first Mars landers. (And, in the spirit of citing sources, I will add that you can find out more about him in William Poundstone's biography, *Carl Sagan: A Life in the Cosmos* [New York: Henry Holt and Company, 1999].) When someone with a background like *that* says that there could be life on Mars, we should listen.

As you explain your source's qualifications, you can also add more evidence to your argument.

> Carol Beckwith, in "Niger's Wodaabe" (*National Geographic* 164, no. 4 [October 1983], pp. 483–509), reports that among the West African Fulani peoples such as the Wodaabe, makeup and clothes are mostly men's business. Beckwith and an anthropologist colleague lived with the Wodaabe for two years and observed many dances for which the men prepared by lengthy preening, face-painting, and teeth-whitening. (Her article includes many pictures too.) Wodaabe women watch, comment, and choose mates for their beauty—which the men say is the natural way. "Our beauty makes the women want us," one says.

Note that an informed source need not fit our general stereotype of an "authority"—and a person who fits our stereotype of an authority may not even be an informed source. If you're checking out colleges, for instance, students are the best authorities, not administrators or recruiters, because it's the students who know what student life is really like. (Just be sure to find yourself a representative sample.)

Note also that authorities on one subject are not necessarily informed about every subject on which they offer opinions.

> Einstein was a pacifist. Therefore, pacifism must be right.

Einstein's genius in physics does not establish him as a genius in political philosophy. Likewise, just because someone can put the title "Doctor" before their name—that is, just because they have a PhD or MD in some field—does not mean that they are qualified to deliver opinions on any subject whatsoever. (Not to name names or anything, but there are some quite prominently cited "Doctors" these days whose doctorates actually have nothing to do with the fields in which they make very self-assured and widely publicized pronouncements.)

Sometimes we must rely on sources whose knowledge is better than ours but still limited in various ways. On occasion, the best information we can get about what is happening in a war zone or a political trial or inside a business or bureaucracy is fragmentary and filtered through journalists, international human rights organizations, corporate watchdogs, and so on. If you must rely on a source that may have limited knowledge in this way, acknowledge the problem. Let your readers or hearers decide whether imperfect authority is better than none at all.

Truly informed sources rarely expect others to accept their conclusions simply because they assert them. Most good sources will offer at least some reasons or evidence—examples, facts, analogies, other kinds of arguments—to help explain and defend their conclusions. Beckwith, for example, offers photographs and stories from the years she lived with the Wodaabe. Sagan wrote whole books explaining space exploration and what we might find beyond Earth. Thus, while we might need to take some of their *specific* claims on authority alone (for instance, we must take Beckwith at her word that she had certain experiences), we can expect even the best sources to offer arguments as well as their own judgments in support of their general conclusions. Look for those arguments, then, and look at them critically as well.

Seek impartial sources

People who have the most at stake in a dispute are usually not the best sources of information about the issues involved. Sometimes they may not even tell the truth. People accused in criminal trials are presumed innocent until proven guilty, but we seldom completely believe their claims of innocence without confirmation from impartial witnesses. Readiness to tell the truth as one sees it, though, is not always enough. The truth as one honestly sees it can still be biased. We tend to see what we expect to see. We notice, remember, and pass on information that supports our point of view, but we may not be quite so motivated when the evidence points the other way.

Therefore, look for *impartial* sources: people or organizations who do not have a stake in the immediate issue, and who have a prior and primary interest in accuracy, such as (some) university scientists or statistical databases. Don't just rely on politicians or interest groups on *one* side of a major public question for the most accurate information about the issues at stake. Don't just rely on manufacturers' advertisements for reliable information concerning their products.

NO:

My car dealer recommends that I pay $300 to rustproof my car. He should know; I guess I'd better do it.

He probably *does* know, but he might not be entirely reliable, either. The best information about consumer products and services comes from independent consumer testing agencies, agencies not affiliated with any manufacturer or provider but answering to consumers who want the most accurate information they can get. Do some research!

YES:

Consumer Reports says that rust problems have almost disappeared in modern cars due to better manufacturing, and advises that dealer rust-proofing is not needed (see "Don't Waste Money on Unnecessary Extras," *Consumer Reports Buying Guide 2006*, p. 153). Therefore, I don't need it!

Likewise, independent service professionals and mechanics are relatively impartial sources of information. For political matters, especially when the disagreements are basically over statistics, look to independent government agencies, such as the Census Bureau, or to university studies or other independent sources. Organizations like Doctors Without Borders are relatively impartial sources on the human rights situation in other countries because they practice medicine, not politics: they are not trying to support or oppose any specific government.

Of course, independence and impartiality are not always easy to judge, either. Be sure that your sources are *genuinely* independent and not just interest groups masquerading under an independent-sounding name. Check who funds them; check their other publications; look for their track record; watch the tone of their statements. Sources that make extreme or simplistic claims, or spend most of their time attacking and demeaning the other side, weaken their own claims. Again, seek out sources that offer constructive arguments and responsibly acknowledge and thoroughly engage the arguments and evidence on the other side. At the very least, try to confirm for yourself any factual claim quoted from a potentially biased source. Good arguments cite their sources (Rule 13); look them up. Make sure the evidence is quoted correctly and not pulled out of context, and check for further information that might be helpful.

16

Cross-check sources

Consult and compare a variety of sources to see if other, equally good authorities agree. Are the experts sharply divided or in agreement? If they're pretty much in agreement, theirs is the safe view to take. (At the very least, if you propose to take a different view, you have some serious explaining to do.) Where even the experts disagree, though, it's best to reserve judgment yourself too. Don't jump in with two feet where truly informed people tread with care. See if you can argue on some other grounds—or rethink your conclusions.

Authorities are most likely to agree about specific, factual matters. That Wodaabe men spend a great deal of time on clothes and makeup is a specific factual claim, for instance, and in principle not hard to verify. On larger and less tangible issues, it is harder to find authorities who agree. Can, or should, the U.S. Constitution be read in terms of the Founders' "original intent"? Do we have free will? Distinguished jurists disagree with each other; great philosophers have held opposing views. You can still quote some of them as authorities if you know that your audience already agrees with them and respects them (but then again, there's always that question: should *you?*). In general, though, do not expect their mere assertions to carry authority. Once again, look to the arguments behind the assertions.

Remember, though: mere disagreement does not automatically disqualify a source. A few people may still disagree that the Earth is round, but it is not a genuinely open question. Likewise, although there was a time when experts disagreed about global climate change, the world scientific community is now nearly unanimous that it is occurring and needs to be addressed.[7] Sure, there's still controversy, but not among the experts. You may need to look into disagreements such as these to decide how seriously to take them.

Use the Web with care

Enter a few keywords and the Web will give you truckloads of information on almost any question or issue. All manner of views and topics are available, almost instantly, that would take forever to turn up if we had to search painstakingly and by hand in libraries or by correspondence.

Reliability, though, is quite another matter. Libraries have at least some checks on the reliability of the books and other materials they collect. Reputable publishers consult the community of experts before presenting any views as expert. Some publishers are even renowned for employing offices of fact-checkers. But on the Web anyone can say anything whatsoever, and with a little skill or money even the flimsiest opinion site can be dressed up to look sober-minded and professional. There are very few checks on the content of Web sites—often no checks at all.

Only rely on Web sources, then, if you are dealing with an identifiable and independently reputable source. Don't rely on a Web site at all unless you have some idea of its source. Key questions are: Who created this site? Why did they create it? What are their qualifications? What does it mean if they don't tell you? How can you double-check and cross-check its claims?

Be aware that Web search engines do not search "everything"—far from it. They search only what is indexed, which is only 10 to 20 percent of the available Web, and heavily weighted toward merchandising and "hot" sites. Especially on controversial issues, where evidence and conclusions are in dispute, the sites that come up first (and often are *designed* to come up first) are likely to be opinionated bluster from nonexperts with agendas. In fact, the best information is often found in databases or

---

[7] See *Climate Change 2007,* Report of the Intergovernmental Panel on Climate Change, a global scientific effort established by the United Nations Environmental Program and the World Meteorological Organization (Cambridge, UK: Cambridge University Press, 2007, and on the Web at http://www.ipcc.ch/).

other academic resources that standard search engines cannot enter at all. Normally you have to search *within* these databases to find the most reliable articles or information on any given topic.

When you really need to know something, then, dig deeper than the standard Web search. What you'll get usually will require harder and more careful reading and thinking—which is what you want, of course—and sometimes a password (hopefully available to you as a student or library patron) in turn. If you are preparing a research project for a class, your teacher should be able to guide you to appropriate Web resources. If not, ask your librarian!

V

Arguments about Causes

Did you know that students who sit at the front of the classroom tend to get better grades? And that people who are married are, on average, happier than people who aren't? Wealth, by contrast, doesn't seem to correlate with happiness at all—so maybe it is true after all that "the best things in life are free." If you'd rather have the money anyway, you might be interested to know that people with "can-do" attitudes tend to be wealthier. So you'd better work on your attitude, eh?

Here we come to arguments about causes and their effects—about what causes what. Such arguments are often vital. Good effects we want to increase, bad effects we want to prevent, and we often want to give appropriate credit or blame for both. It won't surprise you, though, that reasoning about causes also takes care and critical thinking.

18

Causal arguments start with correlations

The evidence for a claim about causes is usually a *correlation*—a regular association—between two events or kinds of events: between your grades in a class and where you sit in the classroom; between being married and being happy; between the unemployment rate and the crime rate, etc. The general form of the argument therefore is:

Event or condition E_1 is *regularly associated* with event or condition E_2.

Therefore, event or condition E_1 *causes* event or condition E_2.

That is, *because* E_1 is regularly associated with E_2 in this way, we conclude that E_1 causes E_2. For example:

People who meditate tend to be calmer.

Therefore, meditation calms you down.

Trends may also be correlated, as when we note that increasing violence on television correlates with increasing violence in the real world.

Shows on television portray more and more violence, callousness, and depravity—and society is becoming more and more violent, callous, and depraved.

Therefore, television is ruining our morals.

Inverse correlations (that is, where an increase in one factor correlates to a *decrease* in another) may suggest causality too. For example, some studies correlate increased vitamin use with decreased health, suggesting that vitamins may (sometimes) be harmful. In the same way, *non*correlation may imply *lack* of cause, as when we discover that happiness and wealth are not correlated and therefore conclude that money does not bring happiness.

Exploring correlations is also a scientific research strategy. What causes lightning? Why do some people become insomniacs, or geniuses, or Republicans? And isn't there *some* way (please?) to prevent colds? Researchers look for correlates to these conditions of interest: that is, for other conditions or events that are regularly associated with lightning or genius or colds, for example, but without which lightning or genius or colds don't tend to happen. These correlates may be subtle and complex, but finding them is often possible nonetheless—and then (hopefully) we have a handle on causes.

Correlations may have alternative explanations

Arguments from correlation to cause are often compelling. However, there is also a systematic difficulty with any such claim. The problem is simply that *any correlation may be explained in multiple ways.* It's often not clear from the correlation itself how best to interpret the underlying causes.

First, some correlations may simply be coincidental. It's not likely that the expanding universe is driving, say, the rise in the price of tomatoes or textbooks. Both the universe and consumer prices continue to inflate, but there is no causal connection.

Second, even when there really is a connection, correlation by itself does not establish the *direction* of the connection. If E_1 is correlated with E_2, E_1 may cause E_2—but E_2 may instead cause E_1. For example, while it is true (on average) that people with "can-do" attitudes tend to be wealthier, it's not at all clear that the attitude leads to the wealth. Surely it is more plausible the other way around: that the wealth causes the attitude. You're more apt to believe in the possibility of success when you've already been successful. Wealth and attitude may correlate, then, but if you want to get wealthier, just working on your attitude is not likely to get you very far.

Likewise, it's entirely possible that calmer people tend to be drawn to meditation, rather than becoming calmer *because* they meditate. And the very same correlation that suggests that television is "ruining our morals" could instead suggest that our morals are ruining television (that is, that rising real-world violence is leading to an increase in the portrayal of violence on television).

Third, some other cause may underlie and explain both of the correlates. Again E_1 may be correlated with E_2, but rather than E_1 causing E_2 *or* E_2 causing E_1, something else—some E_3—may cause both E_1 and E_2. For example, the fact that students who sit in the front of the classroom tend to get better grades may not imply *either* that sitting in the front leads to better grades *or* that getting better grades leads to sitting in the front of the class. More likely, some students' special commitment to making the most of their schooling leads *both* to sitting in the front of the classroom *and* to better grades.

Finally, multiple or complex causes may be at work, and they may move in many directions at the same time. Violence on television, for example, surely reflects a more violent state of society, but also, to some degree, it surely helps to worsen that violence. Quite likely there are other underlying causes as well, such as the breakup of traditional value systems and the absence of constructive pastimes.

Work toward the most likely explanation

Since a variety of explanations for a correlation are usually possible, the challenge for a good correlation-based argument is to find the most *likely* explanation.

First, fill in the connections. That is, spell out how each possible explanation could make sense.

NO:

> Most of my open-minded friends are well read; most of my less open-minded friends are not. I conclude that reading leads to open-mindedness.

YES:

> Most of my open-minded friends are well read; most of my less open-minded friends are not. It makes sense that the more you read, the more you encounter challenging new ideas, ideas that make you less insistent on your own. Reading also lifts you out of your daily world and shows you how different and many-sided life can be. Reading, therefore, leads to open-mindedness.

Try to fill in the connections in this way not just for the explanation you favor, but also for alternative explanations. Consider for example the studies that correlate increased vitamin use with decreased health. One possible explanation is that vitamins actually worsen health, or anyway that some vitamins (or taking a lot of them) are bad for some people. It is also possible, though, that people who already are in bad or worsening health may be using more vitamins to try to get better. In fact, this alternative explanation seems, at least at first glance, equally or even more plausible.

To decide which is the most likely explanation for this correlation, you need more information. In particular, is there other evidence that (some?) vitamins can sometimes be harmful? If so, how widespread might these harms be? If there is little direct and specific evidence of harm to be found, especially when vitamins are taken in appropriate dosages, then it's more likely that poorer health leads to more vitamin use than that more vitamin use leads to poorer health.

Or again: Marriage and happiness correlate (again, on average), but is it because marriage makes you happier or because happier people tend to be more successful at getting and staying married? Fill in the connections for both explanations and then step back to think. Marriage clearly offers companionship and support, which could explain how marriage might make you happier. Conversely, it may be that happy people are better at getting and staying married. To me, though, this second explanation seems less likely. Happiness may make you a more appealing partner, but then again it may not—it could instead make you more self-absorbed— and it is not clear that happiness by itself makes you any more committed or responsive a partner. I'd prefer the first explanation.

Note that the most likely explanation is very seldom some sort of conspiracy or supernatural intervention. It is *possible,* of course, that the Bermuda Triangle really is spooked and that is why ships and planes disappear there. But that explanation is far less likely than another simple and natural explanation: that the Bermuda Triangle is one of the world's heaviest-traveled shipping and sailing areas, with tropical weather that is unpredictable and sometimes severe. Besides, people do tend to embellish spooky stories, so some of the more lurid accounts, having passed through countless retellings, aren't (let's just say) the most reliable. Good fodder for the movies, maybe, but hardly reliable premises for an argument.

Likewise, although people fasten onto inconsistencies and oddities in dramatic events (the JFK assassination, 9/11, etc.) to justify conspiracy theories, such explanations usually leave a great deal more *un*explained than the usual explanations, however incomplete. (For instance, why would any plausible conspiracy take *this particular form?*) Don't assume that every little oddity must have some nefarious explanation. It's hard enough to get the basics right. Neither you nor anyone else needs to have an answer for everything.

Expect complexity

Plenty of happy people are not married, of course, and plenty of married people are unhappy. It does not follow that marriage has no effect on happiness *on average.* It's just that happiness and unhappiness (and, for that matter, being married or unmarried) have a myriad of other causes too. One correlation is not the whole story. The question in such cases is about the *relative weight* of different causes.

If you or someone else has argued that some E_1 causes some E_2, it is not necessarily a counterexample to show that occasionally E_1 doesn't produce E_2, or that another cause entirely may also sometimes produce E_2. The claim is just that E_1 *often* or *usually* produces E_2, and that other causes less commonly do, or that E_1 is among the *major contributors* to E_2, though the full story may involve multiple causes and there may be other major contributors too. There are people who never smoke cigarettes at all and still get lung cancer, and also people who smoke three packs of cigarettes a day and never get it. Both effects are medically intriguing and important, but the fact remains that smoking is the prime cause of lung cancer.

Many different causes may contribute to an overall effect. Though the causes of global climate change are many and varied, for instance, the fact that some of them are natural, such as changes in the sun's brightness, does not show that human contributions therefore have no effect. Once again, the causal story is complex. Many factors are at work. (Indeed, if the sun is *also* contributing to global warming, there's even more reason to try to decrease our contribution.)

Causes and effects may interpenetrate as well. Reading, for instance, surely does lead to open-mindedness. But open-mindedness also leads to reading . . . which creates more open-mindedness in turn. Meanwhile, certain other factors promote both reading *and* open-mindedness, such as going to college, family environment, certain enthusiastic friends always pressing new books on us, and so on . . . but then again, more open-minded people are more likely to go to college and sustain open-minded families and friendships in the first place. Often the most interesting causal stories are *loops!*

VI

Deductive Arguments

Consider this argument:

> If there are no chance factors in chess, then chess is a game of pure skill.
>
> There are no chance factors in chess.
>
> Therefore, chess is a game of pure skill.

Suppose that the premises of this argument are true. In other words, suppose it's true that *if* there are no chance factors in chess, then chess is a game of pure skill—and suppose there *are* no chance factors in chess. You can therefore conclude with perfect assurance that chess is a game of pure skill. There is no way to admit the truth of these premises but deny the conclusion.

Arguments of this type are called *deductive arguments*. That is, a (properly formed) deductive argument is an argument of such a form that if its premises are true, the conclusion must be true too. Properly formed deductive arguments are called *valid* arguments.

Deductive arguments differ from the sorts of arguments so far considered, in which even a large number of true premises does not guarantee the truth of the conclusion (although sometimes they may make it very likely). In nondeductive arguments, the conclusion unavoidably goes beyond the premises—that's the very point of arguing by example, authority, and so on—whereas the conclusion of a valid deductive argument only makes explicit what is already contained in the premises.

In real life, of course, we can't always be sure of our premises either, so the conclusions of real-life deductive arguments still have to be taken with a few (sometimes many) grains of salt. Still, when strong premises can be found, deductive forms are very useful. And even when the premises are uncertain, deductive forms offer an effective way to organize arguments.

Modus ponens

Using the letters **p** and **q** to stand for declarative sentences, the simplest valid deductive form is

> If [sentence **p**] then [sentence **q**].
>
> [Sentence **p**].
>
> Therefore, [sentence **q**].

Or, more briefly:

> If **p** then **q**.
>
> **p.**
>
> Therefore, **q.**

This form is called *modus ponens* ("the mode of putting": put **p**, get **q**). Taking **p** to stand for "There are no chance factors in chess," and **q** to stand for "Chess is a game of pure skill," our introductory example follows *modus ponens* (check it out). Here is another:

> If drivers on cell phones have more accidents, then drivers should be prohibited from using them.
>
> Drivers on cell phones *do* have more accidents.
>
> Therefore, drivers should be prohibited from using cell phones.

To develop this argument, you must explain and defend both of its premises, and they require quite different arguments (go back and look). *Modus ponens* gives you a way to lay them out clearly and separately from the start.

Modus tollens

A second valid deductive form is *modus tollens* ("the mode of taking": take **q**, take **p**).

> If **p** then **q**.
>
> Not-**q**.
>
> Therefore, not-**p**.

Here "Not-**q**" simply stands for the denial of **q**, that is, for the sentence "It is not true that **q**." The same is true for "not-**p**."

Remember Sherlock Holmes's argument, discussed under Rule 1:

> A dog was kept in the stables, and yet, though someone had been in and had fetched out a horse, [the dog] had not barked. . . . Obviously the . . . visitor was someone whom the dog knew well.

Holmes's argument can be put as a *modus tollens:*

> If the visitor were a stranger, then the dog would have barked.
>
> The dog did not bark.
>
> Therefore, the visitor was not a stranger.

To write this argument in symbols, you could use **s** for "The visitor was a stranger" and **b** for "The dog barked."

> If **s** then **b**.
>
> Not-**b**.
>
> Therefore, not-**s**.

"Not-**b**" stands for "The dog did not bark," and "not-**s**" stands for "The visitor was not a stranger." As Holmes puts it, the visitor was someone whom the dog knew well.

24

Hypothetical syllogism

A third valid deductive form is "hypothetical syllogism."

> If **p** then **q**.
>
> If **q** then **r**.
>
> Therefore, if **p** then **r**.

For instance:

> If you study other cultures, then you start to realize the variety of human customs.
>
> If you start to realize the variety of human customs, then you become more tolerant.
>
> Therefore, if you study other cultures, then you become more tolerant.

Using the letters in boldface to stand for the component sentences in this statement, we have:

> If **s** then **v**.
>
> If **v** then **t**.
>
> Therefore, if **s** then **t**.

Hypothetical syllogisms are valid for any number of premises, as long as each premise has the form "If **p** then **q**" and the **q** (called the "consequent") of one premise becomes the **p** (the "antecedent") of the next.

Disjunctive syllogism

A fourth valid deductive form is "disjunctive syllogism."

p or **q**.

Not-**p**.

Therefore, **q**.

Consider, for instance, Bertrand Russell's argument discussed under Rule 2:

Either we hope for progress by improving **m**orals or we hope for progress by improving **i**ntelligence.

We can't hope for progress by improving **m**orals.

Therefore, we must hope for progress by improving **i**ntelligence.

Again using the boldface letters as symbols, this argument goes

m or **i**.

Not-**m**.

Therefore, **i**.

There is one complication. In English the word "or" can have two different meanings. Usually "**p** or **q**" means that at least one of **p** or **q** is true, and possibly both. This is called an "inclusive" sense of the word "or" and is the sense normally assumed in logic. Sometimes, though, we use "or" in an "exclusive" sense, in which "**p** or **q**" means that either **p** or **q** is true but *not* both. "Either they'll come by land or they'll come by sea," for example, suggests that they won't come both ways at once. In that case you might be able to infer that if they come one way, then they're *not* coming the other way (better be sure!).

Disjunctive syllogisms are valid regardless of which sense of "or" is used (check it out). But what *else,* if anything, you may be able to infer from a statement like "**p** or **q**"—in particular, whether you can conclude not-**q** if you also know **p**—depends on the meaning of "or" in the specific "**p** or **q**" premise you are considering. Take care!

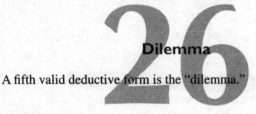

Dilemma

A fifth valid deductive form is the "dilemma."

> **p** or **q**.
>
> If **p** then **r**.
>
> If **q** then **s**.
>
> Therefore, **r** or **s**.

Rhetorically, a dilemma is a choice between two options both of which have unappealing consequences. The pessimist philosopher Arthur Schopenhauer, for example, formulated what is sometimes called the "Hedgehog's dilemma," which we could paraphrase like this:

> The closer two hedgehogs get, the more likely they are to poke each other with their spikes; but if they remain apart, they will be lonely. So it is with people: being close to someone inevitably creates conflicts and provocations and opens us to a lot of pain; but on the other hand, we're lonely when we stand apart.

In outline this argument might be put:

> Either we become close to others or we stand apart.
>
> If we become close to others, we suffer conflict and pain.
>
> If we stand apart, we'll be lonely.
>
> Therefore, either we suffer conflict and pain or we'll be lonely.

And in symbols:

> Either **c** or **a**.
>
> If **c** then **s**.
>
> If **a** then **l**.
>
> Therefore, either **s** or **l**.

A further argument in dilemma form could conclude, even more simply, something like "Either way we'll be unhappy." I'll leave this one to you to write out formally.

Since this is such a jolly little conclusion, maybe I should add that hedgehogs are actually quite able to get close without poking each other. They can be together and comfortable too. Schopenhauer's second premise turns out to be false—at least for hedgehogs.

Reductio ad absurdum

One traditional deductive strategy deserves special mention even though, strictly speaking, it is only a version of *modus tollens.* This is the *reductio ad absurdum,* that is, a "reduction to absurdity." Arguments by *reductio* (or "indirect proof," as they're sometimes called) establish their conclusions by showing that assuming the opposite leads to absurdity: to a contradictory or silly result. Nothing is left to do, the argument suggests, but to accept the conclusion.

To prove: **p.**

Assume the opposite: Not-**p.**

Argue that from the assumption we'd have to conclude: **q.**

Show that **q** *is false (contradictory, "absurd," morally or practically unacceptable . . .).*

Conclude: **p** *must be true after all.*

Rule 12 discussed an argument for the existence of a Creator. Houses have creators, the argument goes, and the world is *like* a house—it too is ordered and beautiful. Thus, the analogy suggests, the world must have a Creator too. Rule 12 also cited David Hume's argument that the world is not relevantly similar enough to a house for this analogy to succeed. In Part V of his *Dialogues,* Hume also suggested a *reductio ad absurdum* of the analogy.[8] Developed, it goes something like this:

> Suppose the world has a Creator like a house does. Now, when houses are not perfect, we know whom to blame: the carpenters and masons who created them. But the world is also not wholly perfect. Therefore, it would seem to follow that the Creator of the world is not perfect either. But you would consider this conclusion absurd. The only way to avoid the absurdity, however, is to reject the supposition that leads to it. Therefore, the world does not have a Creator in the way a house does.

Spelled out in *reductio* form, the argument is:

To prove: The world does not have a Creator in the way a house does.

Assume the opposite: The world does have a Creator in the way a house does.

Argue that from the assumption we'd have to conclude: The Creator is imperfect (because the world is imperfect).

But: God cannot be imperfect.

Conclude: The world does not have a Creator in the way a house does.

Not everyone would find the idea of an imperfect God "absurd," but Hume knew that the Christians with whom he was arguing would not accept it.

---

[8] David Hume, *Dialogues Concerning Natural Religion,* pp. 34–37.

28 Deductive arguments in several steps

Many valid deductive arguments are combinations of the basic forms introduced in Rules 22–27. Here, for example, is Sherlock Holmes performing a simple deduction for Doctor Watson's edification, meanwhile commenting on the relative roles of observation and deduction. Holmes has casually remarked that Watson visited a certain post office that morning, and furthermore that he sent off a telegram while there. "Right!" replies Watson, amazed, "Right on both points! But I confess that I don't see how you arrived at it." Holmes replies:

> "It is simplicity itself. . . . Observation tells me that you have a little reddish mold adhering to your instep. Just opposite the Wigmore Street Post Office they have taken up the pavement and thrown up some earth, which lies in such a way that it is difficult to avoid treading in it in entering. The earth is of this peculiar reddish tint which is found, as far as I know, nowhere else in the neighborhood. So much is observation. The rest is deduction."

> [Watson]: "How, then, did you deduce the telegram?"

> [Holmes]: "Why, of course I knew that you had not written a letter, since I sat opposite to you all morning. I see also in your open desk there that you have a sheet of stamps and a thick bundle of postcards. What could you go into the post office for, then, but to send a wire? Eliminate all other factors, and the one which remains must be the truth."[9]

Putting Holmes's deduction into explicit premises, we might have:

1. Watson has a little reddish mold on his boots.

2. If Watson has a little reddish mold on his boots, then he has been to the Wigmore Street Post Office this morning (because there and only there is reddish dirt of that sort thrown up, and in a way difficult to avoid stepping in).

---

[9] Sir Arthur Conan Doyle, "The Sign of Four," in *The Complete Sherlock Holmes*, pp. 91–92.

3. If Watson has been to the Wigmore Street Post Office this morning, he either mailed a letter, bought stamps or cards, or sent a wire.

4. If Watson had mailed a letter, he would have written the letter this morning.

5. Watson wrote no letter this morning.

6. If Watson had bought stamps or cards, he would not already have a drawer full of stamps and cards.

7. Watson already has a drawer full of stamps and cards.

8. Therefore, Watson sent a wire at the Wigmore Street Post Office this morning.

We now need to break the argument down into a series of valid arguments in the simple forms presented in Rules 22–27. We might start with a *modus ponens:*

2. If Watson has a little reddish mold on his boots, then he has been to the Wigmore Street Post Office this morning.

1. Watson has a little reddish mold on his boots.

I. Therefore, Watson has been to Wigmore Street Post Office this morning.

(I will use I, II, etc. to stand for the conclusions of simple arguments, which then can be used as premises to draw further conclusions.)
Another *modus ponens* follows:

3. If Watson has been to the Wigmore Street Post Office this morning, he either mailed a letter, bought stamps or cards, or sent a wire.

I. Watson has been to Wigmore Street Post Office this morning.

II. Therefore, Watson either mailed a letter, bought stamps or cards, or sent a wire.

Two of these three possibilities now can be ruled out, both by *modus tollens:*

4. If Watson had gone to the post office to mail a letter, he would have written the letter this morning.

5. Watson wrote no letter this morning.

III. Therefore, Watson did not go to the post office to mail a letter.

and

6. If Watson had gone to the post office to buy stamps or cards, he would not already have a drawer full of stamps and cards.

7. Watson already has a drawer full of stamps and cards.

IV. Therefore, Watson did not go to the post office to buy stamps or cards.

Finally we can put it all together:

II. Watson either mailed a letter, bought stamps or cards, or sent a wire at the Wigmore Street Post Office this morning.

III. Watson did not mail a letter.

IV. Watson did not buy stamps or cards.

8. Therefore, Watson sent a wire at the Wigmore Street Post Office this morning.

This last inference is an extended disjunctive syllogism: "Eliminate all other factors, and the one which remains must be the truth."

VII

Extended Arguments

Now suppose that you have picked, or been assigned, an issue or question on which to work out an argumentative essay or oral presentation. Maybe you're writing for a class; maybe you're about to speak at a public forum or write a Letter to the Editor; maybe you're just fascinated by the issue and want to figure out what you think.

To do this you need to go beyond the short arguments we have so far considered. You must work out a more detailed line of thought, in which the main ideas are laid out clearly and their own premises in turn are spelled out and defended. Anything you say requires evidence and reasons, which in turn may take some research, and you will need to weigh arguments for opposing views as well. All of this is hard work, but it is also good work. For many people, in fact, it is one of the most rewarding and enjoyable kinds of thinking there is!

29 Explore the issue

You begin with an issue but not necessarily a position. Do not feel that you must immediately embrace some position and then try to shore it up with arguments. Likewise, even if you have a position, do not just dash off the first argument that occurs to you. You are not being asked for the first opinion that occurs to you. You are being asked to *arrive* at a well-informed opinion that you can defend with solid arguments.

Is life likely on other planets? Carl Sagan says that it is—but why? How could he, or we, argue the point? Here is one line of thought that some astronomers suggest. There are billions of stars in our galaxy alone—and billions of galaxies in the universe. If even a tiny fraction of all these stars have solar systems of their own, and even a tiny fraction of those have planets suitable for life, and even a tiny fraction of *those* actually *have* life, still there must be a myriad of planets with life. The number of chances would still be unimaginably huge.[10]

Then again, why do some people have doubts? Find out. Some scientists point out that we really have no idea how common habitable planets might be, or how likely life is to develop on them. It's all guesswork.[11] Other critics argue that life elsewhere (or rather, intelligent life) by now should have announced itself, which (they say) hasn't happened.

All of these arguments carry some weight, and clearly much more must be said. You already see, then, that unexpected facts or perspectives may well turn up as you research and develop your argument. Be ready to be surprised. Be ready to hear evidence and arguments for positions you may not like. Be ready, even, to let yourself be swayed. True thinking is an open-ended process. The whole point is that you don't know when you start where you'll find yourself in the end.

Even if you have been assigned not just a topic but a position on that topic, you still need to look at arguments for a variety of other views—if only to be prepared to respond to them—and very likely you still have a lot of leeway about how to develop and defend the view you're given. On the most contentious issues, for example, you do not need to roll out the same arguments that everyone has heard a thousand times already. In fact, please don't! Look for creative new approaches. You could even try to find common ground with the other side. In short, take the time to choose your direction carefully, and aim to make some real progress on the issue, even (if you must) from within "given" positions.

---

[10] For a contemporary presentation of this argument, see Donald Goldsmith and Tobias Owen, *The Search for Life in the Universe,* 3rd ed. (Sausalito, CA: University Science Books, 2002), Chapter 17.
[11] You can find a thorough and historical summary of many sides of this discussion in Steven J. Dick, *Life on Other Worlds: The 20th-Century Extraterrestrial Life Debate* (New York: Cambridge University Press, 1998), Chapters 3 and 6.

Spell out basic ideas as arguments

Now remember that you are constructing *arguments:* that is, specific conclusions backed by evidence and reasons. As you begin to formulate a position, take its basic idea and frame it as an argument. Get out a large sheet of scratch paper and literally draft your premises and conclusion in outline.

Aim first for a relatively short argument—say, three to five premises—using the forms offered in this book. The basic argument just introduced for life on other planets, for example, might be put into premises-and-conclusion form in this way:

> Other planets and solar systems are being discovered beyond our own.
>
> If there are other solar systems beyond our own, then it is very probable that there are other planets like Earth.
>
> If there are other planets like Earth, then it is very probable that some of them have life.
>
> Therefore, it is very probable that there is life on some other planets.

For practice, work this argument out as a deductive argument using *modus ponens* and hypothetical syllogism.

For a second example, consider a quite different topic. Some people have recently proposed a major expansion of student exchange programs. Many more young Americans should have the chance to go abroad, they say, and many more young people from other parts of the world should have the chance to come here. It would cost money, of course, and would take some adjustment all around, but a more cooperative and peaceful world might result.

Suppose you want to develop and defend this proposal. First, again, sketch out the main argument for it—the basic idea. Why would people propose (and be so passionate about) expanding student exchange programs?

FIRST TRY:

> Students who travel abroad learn to appreciate different countries.

More appreciation between different countries would be good.

Therefore, we should send more students abroad.

This outline does capture a basic idea, but in truth it is a little *too* basic. It hardly says enough to be much more than a simple assertion. Why, for example, would more appreciation between different countries be good? And how does sending students abroad produce it? Even a basic argument can be worked out a little further.

BETTER:

Students who travel abroad learn to appreciate other countries.

Students who travel abroad become person-to-person ambassadors who help their hosts appreciate the students' home countries.

More appreciation both ways will help us better coexist and cooperate in our interdependent world.

Therefore, we should send more students abroad.

You may have to try several different conclusions—even quite varied conclusions—before you find your best basic argument on a topic. Even after you have settled on the conclusion you want to defend, you may have to try several forms of argument before you find a form that really works well. (I am serious about that *large* sheet of scratch paper!) Again, use the rules in the earlier chapters of this book. Take your time—and give yourself time to take.

Defend basic premises with arguments of their own

Once you have spelled out your basic idea as an argument, it will need defense and development. For anyone who disagrees—in fact, for anyone who doesn't know much about the question in the first place—most of the basic premises will need supporting arguments of their own. Each premise therefore becomes the conclusion of a further argument that you need to work out.

Look back, for example, at the argument about life on other planets (p. 51). The argument begins with the premise that solar systems are already being discovered beyond our solar system. This you can show by citing the scientific literature and news reports.

As of 8 February 2008, the Paris Observatory's "Extrasolar Planet Encyclopaedia" lists 270 known planets of other stars, including 26 in multi-planet systems (http://exoplanet.eu/).

Therefore, other solar systems are being discovered beyond our own.

The second premise of the basic argument for life on other planets is that *if* there are other solar systems beyond our own, then it is very probable that some of them include planets like Earth. Well, how do we know this? What's the supporting argument? Here you probably need to draw on factual knowledge and/or research. If you've paid attention to those same news reports, you have some good reasons to offer. The usual argument is an analogy:

Our own solar system has a variety of kinds of planets, from gas giants to smaller rocky and watery planets suitable for life.

As far as we know, other solar systems will be *like* ours.

Therefore, it is very probable that other solar systems also contain a variety of planets, including some suitable for life.

Continue in this way for all the premises of your basic argument. Once again, it may take some work to find appropriate evidence for each premise that needs defense, and you may even find yourself changing some premises, and therefore the basic argument itself, so that they can be adequately supported by the kinds of evidence you end up finding. This is as it should be! Good arguments are usually in "flow," and each part depends on the others. It's a learning experience.

You'd need to approach the basic argument for student exchange programs in the same way. Why do you think, for instance—and how will you persuade others—that students who go abroad learn to appreciate other cultures? Examples would help, including perhaps the results of surveys or studies you can find through research or by consulting the experts (people who actually run student exchange programs, or social scientists). Again, in some way or other, you need to fill in the argument. The same goes for the second basic premise: how do we know that students abroad really do become "person-to-person ambassadors"?

The third basic premise (the value of mutual appreciation) may be more obvious, and in some quick arguments you could reasonably leave it undeveloped. (A point to remember: not *every* premise of your basic argument necessarily needs development and defense.) However, it is also a fine occasion to make the force of the argument—the expected benefits —more vivid. Maybe this way:

> Appreciation leads us to see virtues in others' ways, and to expect virtues even when we don't see them yet.
>
> Appreciation is also a form of enjoyment: it enriches our own experience.
>
> When we see or expect virtues in others' ways, and find that they enrich our own experience, we are less tempted to make harsh or single-minded judgments about them, and we can work with them more readily.
>
> Therefore, mutual appreciation will help us better coexist and cooperate in our interdependent world.

Add some concrete examples to fill out these premises in turn, and you'll have yourself a fine argument overall.

32
Consider objections

Too often, when we make arguments, we concern ourselves only with the *pro* side: what can be said in support. Objections tend to come as a shock. We realize, maybe a little late, that we didn't think enough about possible problems. It's better to do so yourself and to hone your argument— maybe even make fundamental changes—in advance. In this way, you also make it clear to your eventual audience that you have done your homework, that you have explored the issue thoroughly and (hopefully!) with a somewhat open mind. So always ask: What are the best arguments *against* the conclusion you are working on?

Most actions have *many* effects, not just one. Maybe some of the other effects—ones you haven't looked at yet—are less desirable. Thoughtful and well-meaning people may oppose even such obviously good ideas ("obvious" to us, anyway) as taking ourselves in for regular checkups or getting married in order to be happy or sending more students abroad. Try to anticipate and honestly consider their concerns.

Students abroad, for example, may also end up in dangerous situations, and bringing large numbers of new foreign students here might raise national security risks. And all of it might cost a lot of money. These are important objections. On the other hand, perhaps they can be answered. Maybe you'll want to argue that the costs are worth it, for example, in part because there are also costs of *not* reaching out to other cultures. After all, we are already sending large numbers of young people —in the military—into extreme danger abroad. You could argue that giving ourselves another and different face abroad might be a very good investment.

Other objections may lead you to rethink your proposal or argument. In this case, for example, worries about national security might require us to be careful about who is invited to come here. Clearly they need to come—how else are we going to correct false impressions?—but (you could argue) it may be fair to impose certain restrictions too.

Maybe you are making some general or philosophical claim: that humans have (or don't have) free will, for example, or that war is (or isn't) inherent in human nature, or that there is (or isn't) life on other planets. Here too, anticipate objections. If you are writing an academic paper, look for criticisms of your claim or interpretation in the class readings, secondary texts, or (good) online sources. Talk to people who have different views. Sift through the concerns and objections that come up, pick the strongest and most common ones, and try to answer them. And don't forget to re-evaluate your own argument. Do your premises or conclusion need to be changed or developed to take account of the objections?

33

Consider alternatives

If you are defending a proposal, it is not enough to show that your proposal will solve a problem. You must also show that it is better than other plausible ways of solving that same problem.

Durham's swimming pools are overcrowded, especially on weekends.
Therefore, Durham needs to build more pools.

This argument is weak in several ways. "Overcrowded" is vague, for one
thing: who decides when there are too many people in a pool? But rem-
edying this weakness still will not justify the conclusion. There may be
other and more reasonable ways to address the (possible) problem. Maybe
the existing pools could have more open-swim hours so that swimmers
could spread themselves over more available times. Maybe the typically
lighter-use times could be more widely publicized. Maybe swim meets
and other closed-pool activities could be moved to the weekdays. Or
maybe Durham should do nothing at all and let users adjust their swim
schedules for themselves. If you still want to argue that Durham should
build more pools, you must show that your proposal is better than any of
these (far less expensive) alternatives.

Considering alternatives is not just a formality. The point is not just to
quickly survey a few boringly obvious, easily countered alternatives and
then (big surprise!) to re-embrace your original proposal. Look for serious alternatives, and get creative. You might even come up with something quite new. How about . . . maybe keeping the pools open around the
clock? How about putting in an evening smoothie bar or the like and en-
ticing some of the day swimmers to come at odd hours instead?

If you come up with something really good, you might even need to
change your conclusion. Are there possibly much better ways to organize foreign exchange programs, for instance? Maybe we should extend
such opportunities to all sorts of people, not just students. How about exchange programs for *elders?* Why not for families, congregations, or
work groups? Then it's not just about "sending students abroad" anymore
. . . so it's back to your scratch paper to recast the basic argument. This is
how real thinking works.

Even general or philosophical claims have alternatives. Some people
argue, for instance, that there are not likely to be other civilizations elsewhere in the universe, because if there were, surely we'd have heard from
them by now. But is the premise true? Aren't there other possibilities?
Maybe they *are* out there but are just listening. Maybe they choose to keep
still, or just aren't interested, or are "civilized" in some other direction and
do not have the technology. Maybe they are trying to communicate but not
in the ways we are listening for. It's a very speculative question, but the
existence of alternative possibilities like these does weaken the objection.

Many scientists also think, by the way, that life could arise on planets very different from Earth—it would just be a very different form of life. This is an alternative possibility too, and difficult to judge, but one that you could use to support and even extend the basic argument. Suppose life could be even more widespread than the basic argument suggests?

VIII

Argumentative Essays

Suppose now that you have explored your issue, outlined a basic argument, and defended its premises. You are ready to go public—maybe by writing an argumentative essay.

Remember that actually writing an argumentative essay is the *last* stage! If you have just picked up this book and opened it to this chapter, reflect: there is a reason that this is the eighth chapter and not the first. As the proverbial country Irishman said when a tourist asked him how to get to Dublin, "If you want to get to Dublin, don't start here."

Remember too that the rules in Chapters I–VI apply to writing an essay as well as to writing short arguments. Review the rules in Chapter I in particular. Be concrete and concise, build on substance and not overtone, and so forth. What follow are some additional rules specific to writing argumentative essays.

34 Jump right in

Launch straight into the real work. No windy windups or rhetorical padding.

NO:

For centuries, philosophers have debated the best way to be happy. . . .

We knew that already. Get to *your* point.

YES:

In this essay I will try to show that the best things in life really *are* free.

Make a definite claim or proposal

If you are making a proposal, be specific. "Something should be done" is not a real proposal. You need not be elaborate. "Cell phones should be banned while driving" is a specific proposal but also a very simple one. If you want to argue that the United States should expand study-abroad programs, though, the idea is more complex and therefore needs some elaboration.

Similarly, if you are making a philosophical claim or defending your interpretation of a text or event, begin by stating your claim or interpretation *simply.*

Very probably there is life on other planets.

That's forthright and clear!

Academic essays may aim simply to assess some of the arguments for or against a claim or proposal. You may not be making a claim or proposal of your own or even arriving at a specific decision. For example, you may be able to examine only one line of argument in a controversy. If so, make it clear immediately that this is what you are doing. Sometimes your conclusion may be simply that the arguments for or against some position or proposal are inconclusive. Fine—but make that conclusion clear immediately. You don't want your own essay to seem inconclusive!

Your argument is your outline

You now move to the main body of your essay: your argument. First, just summarize it. Take the basic argument you've outlined and put it into a concise paragraph.

> Many solar systems are now being discovered beyond our own. I will argue that many of them are likely to include planets like Earth. Many of these planets in turn are likely to have life. Very probably, then, there is life on other planets.

Here your aim is just to give the reader the big picture: a clear overview of where you are going and how you propose to get there.

An argumentative essay should now advance each of the premises of this basic argument in turn, each with a paragraph that begins with a re-statement of the premise and continues by developing and defending it.

> Consider first the remarkable fact that many other solar systems are being discovered beyond our own. As of 8 February 2008, the Paris Observatory's "Extrasolar Planet Encyclopaedia" lists 270 known planets of other stars, including 26 in multi-planet systems (http://exoplanet.eu/). . . .

You might go on to discuss a few examples—say, the most recent and intriguing discoveries. In a longer essay, you might cite other lists too, and/or explain the methods being used to discover these planets—it depends on how much room you have and the level of detail and support your readers need or expect. Then go on to explain and defend your other basic premises in the same way.

Some premises in your basic argument may need fairly involved defenses. Treat them exactly the same way. First state the premise you are defending and remind your readers of its role in your main argument. Next summarize your argument for that premise in turn (that is, treating it now as the conclusion of a further argument). Then spell out that argument, giving a paragraph or so, in order, to each of *its* premises.

For instance, in the last chapter (Rule 31) we developed a defense of the second premise of the basic argument for life on other planets. You could insert it now in paragraph form and with a little more style.

> Why might we think that other solar systems include planets like Earth? Astronomers propose an intriguing argument by analogy. They point out that our own solar system has a variety of kinds of planets— some huge gas giants, some others rocky and well suited for liquid water and life. As far as we know, they continue, other solar systems will be *like* ours. Therefore, they conclude, other solar systems very

probably contain a variety of planets, including some that are rocky
and well suited for liquid water and life.

Now you may need to explain and defend these points in turn, maybe even
giving some of them their own paragraph or two each. You could try to
awaken your readers' appreciation for the diversity of planets right here
in our solar system, for example, or describe some of the variety of extrasolar planets already known.

Depending on how long and involved all of this gets, you may need to
reorient your reader to the basic argument when you return to it. Pull out
the road map, as it were, and remind your readers—and yourself—where
you are in your journey toward the main conclusion.

> We have seen, then, that solar systems are already being discovered
> beyond our own, and that it seems very probable that there are other
> planets like Earth. The last main premise of the argument is this: if
> there are other planets like Earth, then very probably some of them
> have life.

In your outline you will have worked out an argument for this premise
too, and you can now bring it smoothly up to bat.

Notice, in all of these arguments, the importance of using consistent
terms (Rule 6). Clearly connected premises such as these become the par-
allel sentences or phrases that hold the whole essay together.

37 Detail objections and meet them

Rule 32 asks you to think about and rework your argument in light of possible objections. Detailing and responding to them in your essay helps to
make your views more persuasive to your readers, and attests that you
have thought carefully about the issue.

NO:

> Someone might object that expanded student exchange programs will
> create too many risks for students. But *I* think that . . .

Well, what kinds of risks? Why would such risks arise? Spell out the
reasons behind the objection. Take the time to sketch the whole counter-

argument, not just to mention its conclusion as you rush by to defend *your* argument.

YES:

> Someone might object that expanded student exchange programs will create too many risks for students. The concern is partly, I think, that students abroad, who are mostly young people, after all, and not so worldly, may be more easily taken advantage of or hurt, especially in places where life is more desperate and there are fewer safeguards and protections.
>
> In this time of rising fear and mistrust of foreigners, coupled with fears of terrorism, the concern may also take on more of an edge: students' lives may be at stake. We would certainly not want exchange students to become hostages in desperate local power games. Western tourists abroad are already sometimes targeted by terrorists; we could justifiably fear that the same might happen to exchange students.
>
> These are serious concerns. Still, equally serious responses are also possible. . . .

Now it is clear exactly what the objections are, and you can try to respond to them effectively. You might point out, for instance, that risks don't just start at the border. Many foreign countries are safer than American cities. A more complex response might be that it is also risky, at least to our society as a whole, *not* to send more cultural ambassadors abroad, since international misunderstandings and the hatreds they fuel are making the world more risky for all of us. And surely there are creative ways to design exchange programs to reduce some of the risks? You might not even have thought of these possibilities, though, if you had not detailed the arguments behind the objection, and your readers would probably not have seen the point even if you had mentioned them. Detailing the objections enriches *your* argument in the end.

Get feedback and use it

Maybe you know exactly what you mean. Everything seems clear to you. However, it may be far from clear to anyone else! Points that seem connected to you may seem completely unrelated to someone reading your essay. I have seen students hand in an essay that they think is sharp and clear only to find, when they get it back, that they themselves can barely understand what they were thinking when they wrote it. Their grades usually aren't too encouraging either.

Writers—at all levels—need *feedback*. It is through others' eyes that you can see best where you are unclear or hasty or just plain implausible. Feedback improves your logic too. Objections may come up that you hadn't expected. Premises you thought were secure may turn out to need defending, while other premises may turn out to be more secure than they seemed. You may even pick up a few new facts or examples. Feedback is a "reality check" all the way around—welcome it.

Some teachers build student feedback on paper drafts right into the timetable of their classes. If your teacher does not, arrange it yourself. Find willing fellow students and exchange drafts. Go to your campus Writing Center (yes, you do have one—you may just need to look for it). Encourage your readers to be critical, and commit yourself to being a critical reader for them in turn. If need be, you might even assign your readers a quota of specific criticisms and suggestions to make, so they don't fear hurting your feelings by suggesting some. It may be polite but it really does *not* do you a favor if your would-be critics just glance over your writing and reassure you that it is lovely, whatever it says. Your teacher and eventual audience will not give you such a free pass.

We may underrate feedback partly because we typically don't see it at work. When we only read finished pieces of writing—essays, books, magazines—it can be easy to miss the fact that writing is essentially a *process*. The truth is that every single piece of writing you read is put together by someone who starts from scratch and makes thousands of choices and multiple revisions along the way. This very book you hold in your hands has gone through at least twenty drafts throughout its four editions, with formal and informal feedback from dozens and dozens of people. Development, criticism, clarification, and change are the keys. Feedback is what makes them go.

39

Modesty, please!

Don't claim more than you've shown.

NO:

In sum, every reason favors sending more students abroad, and none of the objections stands up at all. What are we waiting for?

YES:

In sum, there is an appealing case for sending more students abroad. Although uncertainties may remain, on the whole it seems to be a promising step. It's worth a try.

Maybe the second version overdoes it in the other direction, but you see the point. Very seldom will you put all the objections to rest, and anyway the world is an uncertain place. We're not experts, most of us, and even the experts can be wrong. "It's worth a try" is the best attitude.

IX

Oral Arguments

Sometimes you will find yourself arguing in face-to-face public settings: debating in front of a class; arguing for a bigger share of the student government budget or speaking for your neighborhood at City Council; invited to make a presentation on a subject of your interest or expertise by a group that is interested. Sometimes your audience will be friendly, sometimes they will be neutral but willing to listen, and sometimes they will really need to be won over. At all times, you'll want to present good arguments effectively.

All of the rules in the earlier chapters of this book apply to oral arguments as well as argumentative essays. Here are a few further rules for oral arguments in particular.

40

Reach out to your audience

In making an oral argument you are quite literally asking for a *hearing*. You want to be heard: to be listened to with respect and at least some degree of open-mindedness. But your hearers may or may not start out respectful or open-minded, and may not even bring a genuine interest in your topic. You need to reach out to them to create the kind of hearing you want to have.

One way to reach out is through your own enthusiasm. Bring some of your own interest and energy for the topic into your talk early on. It personalizes you and notches up the energy in the room.

> I appreciate the chance to speak to you today. In this talk, I want to put
> forward a new idea on the subject of student exchange programs. It's

a proposal I find exciting and inspiring, and I'm hoping that, by the end, you will too.

Notice also that this way of talking itself displays the respectful and inviting attitude toward your hearers that you'd like them to take toward you. You may not get it back from them, even so—but you certainly won't get it from them if you don't bring it to them in the first place. Arguing face to face can be a powerful thing, and done deftly and persistently, it can reinforce and build respect itself, even across major differences.

Patience is helpful too—and again, *show* it. If your aim is to persuade your audience of a view they currently do not accept, do not act as though they should immediately change their minds and rise as one to agree with you. People typically don't work that way. Instead, just ask for their open-minded consideration. Expect them to be *willing to consider* changing (and of course, again, you will be most successful at this if you are visibly willing to consider changing yourself). Pushing harder may just bring up those unpleasant stereotypes of "argument" that drive people further into rigid thinking.

Never give an audience the feeling that you are talking down to them. They may know less than you do about the subject, but they can certainly learn, and it is pretty likely that you have some learning to do too. You're not there to rescue them from their ignorance, but rather to share some new information or ideas that you hope they'll find as intriguing and suggestive as you do. Again, approach your audience from *enthusiasm,* not some sort of superiority.

Respect your audience, then, and also respect yourself. You are there because you have something to offer, and they are there either because they want to hear it or because it is required by their jobs or studies. You do not need to apologize for taking their time. Just thank them for listening, and use the time well.

Be fully present

A public talk or speech is a face-to-face occasion. It is not simply a public version of what we do privately when we read. After all, if people just wanted your words, reading would be much more efficient. They are there partly for your *presence.*

So, be present! For starters, look at your audience. Take the time to connect. Meet people's eyes and hold them. People who get nervous speaking to groups are sometimes advised to talk to one person in the group, as if one to one. Do so, if you need to, but then go a step further: talk to your whole audience one to one, one person at a time.

Speak with expression. Do not read your pre-prepared words as if it were a chore. Remember, you're *talking* to people here! Imagine that you are having an animated conversation with a friend (OK, maybe a little one-sided . . .). Now speak to your audience in the same spirit.

Writers seldom get to see their readers. When you speak in public, though, your hearers are right there in front of you, and you have constant feedback from them. Use it. Do people meet your eyes with interest? What is the feeling in the audience as a whole? Are people leaning forward to hear better . . . or not? If not, can you pick up the energy? Even if you have a presentation to get through, you can still adjust your style, or stop to explain or review a key point if necessary. When you are not sure of your audience, plan in advance to be able to adjust to different responses. Have an extra story or illustration ready to go, just in case.

By the way, you are not glued to the floor behind the podium (should you have one). You can walk around or at least come out from behind the lectern. Depending on your own comfort level and the occasion, you can establish a much more engaged feeling in the room by visibly engaging with your audience yourself.

Signpost your argument

Readers can take in an argument selectively. They can stop and think, double back, or choose to drop it entirely and move on to something else. Your listeners can't do any of these things. You set the pace for everyone.

So be considerate. On the whole, oral arguments need to offer more "signposting" and repetition than written arguments. At the beginning, you may need to summarize the argument more fully, and then you need to refer more regularly back to the summary, or what Rule 36 called the "road map." For your summary, use labels like "Here is my basic argument." For your premises, as the argument turns, say something like, "We come now to the second [third, fourth, etc.] basic premise of my argument. . . ." Summarize again at the end. Pause to mark important transitions and to give people time to think.

In my college debate training I was taught to literally repeat my key claims word for word—that's right, to literally repeat my key claims word for word—mainly because other people were writing them down. Sometimes I still do this as a teacher: it shows that you know people are listening hard and that they may want and need the key points signposted. In other settings, this might seem odd. Even if you don't repeat the key points word for word, at least mark them out in some way, and make it clear that—and why—you are doing so.

Be especially alert to your audience at important transitions. Look around and make sure that most of your hearers are ready to move with you. You'll communicate better and show your audience that you actually care that they take in and understand what you are saying.

Offer something positive

Offer your audience something to do, something to hope for, some sense of possibility—at least some kind of positive spin.

NO:

> This city stinks at conserving water! Even with the reservoirs down to a month's supply, we've only been able to cut back consumption by 25 percent, and people still don't get it about not washing their cars or leaving their sprinklers going forever. . . .

Maybe, maybe . . . But when we focus on the severity of a problem, we also run the risk of making people feel like nothing can be done about it. Couldn't the same issue be framed in a more empowering way?

YES:

> This city needs to do better at conserving water. We've been able to cut back consumption by 25 percent so far, but with the reservoirs down to a month's supply, people should really start seeing the need to stop washing their cars or leaving their sprinklers going. . . .

These are exactly the same facts, even similar phrases and sentences, but the overall feeling is sharply different.

The point is not to be mindlessly optimistic. We should not ignore what is negative. But when we let it fill the screen entirely, it becomes the only reality. We create more of it, we preoccupy ourselves with it, and it gets our energy and attention, even if we wish to resist it.

Instead, give your audience some direction forward, some way to respond, something to do, not just something to resist or avoid or lament. Part of the power of Martin Luther King, Jr.'s famous "I Have a Dream" speech is that it is, after all, about *dreams:* about positive visions for a shared and just future. "I have a dream that the children of former slaves and the children of former slave-owners will be able to sit down together at the table of brotherhood. . . ." Imagine if he'd spoken only about nightmares instead: "I have a *nightmare* that the children of former slaves and the children of former slave-owners will *never* be able to sit down together at the table of brotherhood. . . ." In one way this is exactly the same idea—but if King had put it this way, would his great speech live on today?

All arguments—not just oral arguments—should try to offer something positive. Again, though, there is a special energy in oral arguments, which is why I place this rule in this chapter. An audience's optimism and excitement can be infectious, and it can become a power of its own, as can a sense of gloom and disempowerment. Which will you choose to create?

Use visual aids sparingly

PowerPoint has become a familiar accompaniment to visual presentations. Some people even expect to read presentations from computer projectors as a matter of course.

Nonetheless, audiences may quickly tire of seeing totally different subjects all presented in the same way, often using the very same backgrounds and formats. Then too, PowerPoint can make it too easy to think that you've got "content" when mostly what you have is just a nicely decorated presentation. Critics have also pointed out that PowerPoint formats tend to oversimplify. The writing on slides typically is very clipped; charts and graphs can display little detail. And computer glitches inevitably lead to distractions and sometimes total disasters.

So think carefully about what kinds of visual aids you really need—if any. Learn PowerPoint if you have to (students going into business may need it), but do not assume that it is the only way to make a presentation. Try for something more engaging and fully focused. Perhaps you can ask for a show of hands on some subject, or solicit some structured audience participation. Read briefly from a book or article. Put up a short video clip or some graphs or data, if needed, but then turn the screen off to continue talking. At the very least, don't let your presentation be reduced to a tour through some slides—for that can be done just as well, or better, without *you*.

If you really want or need to use visual aids, consider paper handouts. You can include far more information—complex words and pictures; graphs, data, references, links—including much that can be left for people to read before or after the presentation if they choose. Distribute your handouts in advance, or only when you are ready to use them, or for reference at the end, and encourage people to take them when they go.

End in style

First, end on time. Find out how long you are supposed to speak, and don't go over. You know from your own experiences as a listener that nothing irritates an audience more than a speaker who goes on too long.

Second, don't just peter out.

NO:

Well, I guess that's about all the time I have. Why don't we stop and chat a bit if any of these ideas have interested you?

Come to a rousing end. End in style, with flair or a flourish.

YES:

In this talk I have tried to suggest that real happiness is attainable after all, and by everyone; that it takes no special luck or wealth; indeed that its preconditions lie within easy reach, all around us. I thank you for your attention, my friends, and naturally wish you all the greatest happiness yourselves!

Appendix I

Some Common Fallacies

Fallacies are misleading types of arguments. Many of them are so tempting, and therefore so common, that they even have their own names. This may make them seem like a separate and new topic. Actually, though, to call something a fallacy is usually just another way of saying that it violates one of the rules for *good* arguments. The fallacy of "false cause," for example, is a questionable conclusion about causes, and you can look to Chapter V for explanation.

Here is a short list and explanation of some of the classical fallacies, including their Latin names when frequently used.

ad hominem (literally, "to the man"):   attacking the *person* of a source rather than his or her qualifications or reliability, or the actual argument he or she makes. You know from Chapter IV that supposed authorities may be disqualified if they are not informed, impartial, or largely in agreement. But other sorts of attacks on supposed authorities are typically not legitimate.

> It's no surprise that Carl Sagan argues for life on Mars—after all, he was a well-known atheist. I don't believe it for a minute.

Alhough Sagan did take part in the public discussion about religion and science, there is no reason to think that his views about religion colored his scientific judgment about Martian life. Look to the argument, not "the man."

ad ignorantiam (appeal to ignorance):   arguing that a claim is true just because it has not been shown to be false. A classic example is this state-

ment by Senator Joseph McCarthy when he was asked for evidence to
back up his accusation that a certain person was a Communist:

> I do not have much information on this except the general statement
> of the agency that there is nothing in the files to disprove his Commu-
> nist connections.

ad misericordiam (appeal to pity):   appealing to pity as an argument for
special treatment.

> I know I flunked every exam, but if I don't pass this course, I'll have
> to retake it in summer school. You *have* to let me pass!

Pity is sometimes a good reason to help, but it is certainly inappropriate
when objective evaluation is called for.

ad populum: appealing to the emotions of a crowd; also, appealing to a
person to go along with the crowd ("Everyone's doing it!"). Arguments
ad populum are good examples of *bad* arguments from authority. No reasons are offered to show that "everybody" is any kind of knowledgeable
or reliable source.

affirming the consequent: a deductive mistake of the form

> If **p** then **q**.
>
> **q**.
>
> Therefore, **p**.

Remember that in the statement "if **p** then **q**," **p** is called the "antecedent"
and **q** the "consequent." The second premise of *modus ponens*—a valid
form—affirms (asserts) the antecedent, **p** (go back to Rule 22 and check).
Affirming the consequent (**q**), though, yields quite a different—and
invalid—form. A true conclusion is not guaranteed even if the premises
are true. For example:

> When the roads are icy, the mail is late.

The mail is late.

Therefore, the roads are icy.

Although the mail would be late if the roads were icy, it may be late for other reasons too. This argument **overlooks alternatives.**

begging the question: implicitly using your conclusion as a premise.

God exists because it says so in the Bible, which I know is true because God wrote it, after all!

To put this argument in premise-and-conclusion form, you'd have to write:

The Bible is true, because God wrote it.

The Bible says that God exists.

Therefore, God exists.

To defend the claim that the Bible is true, the arguer claims that God wrote it. But, obviously, if God wrote the Bible, then God exists. Thus the argument assumes just what it is trying to prove.

circular argument: same as **begging the question.**

You can count on WARP News for the facts, because they constantly say on the air that "we just give you the facts," so that must be a fact too!

Real-life circular arguments often follow a bigger circle, but they all eventually end up starting in the same place they want to end.

complex question: posing a question in such a way that people cannot agree *or* disagree with you without committing themselves to some other claim you wish to promote. A simple example: "Are you still as self-centered as you used to be?" Answering either "yes" or "no" commits you to agreeing that you used to be self-centered. A more subtle example: "Will you follow your conscience instead of your pocketbook and donate to the cause?" Saying "no," regardless of their real reasons for not donating, makes people feel guilty. Saying "yes," regardless of their real reasons for donating, makes them noble. If you want a donation, just ask for it.

denying the antecedent: a deductive mistake of the form

If **p** then **q**.

Not-**p**.

Therefore, not-**q**.

Remember that, in the statement "If **p** then **q**," **p** is called the "antecedent" and **q** the "consequent." The second premise of a *modus tollens*—a valid form—denies the consequent, **q** (go back to Rule 23 and check). Denying the antecedent (**p**), though, yields quite a different—and invalid— form. A true conclusion is not guaranteed even if the premises are true. For example:

When the roads are icy, the mail is late.

The roads are not icy.

Therefore, the mail is not late.

Although the mail would be late if the roads were icy, it may be late for other reasons too. This argument **overlooks alternatives.**

equivocation: sliding from one meaning of a term to another in the middle of an argument.

Women and men are physically and emotionally different. The sexes are *not* "equal," then, and therefore the law should not pretend that we are.

Between premise and conclusion this argument shifts the meaning of the term "equal." The sexes are not physically and emotionally "equal" in the sense in which "equal" means simply "identical." Equality before the law, however, does not mean "physically and emotionally identical" but "entitled to the same rights and opportunities." Rephrased with the two different senses of "equal" made clear, the argument goes:

> Women and men are not physically and emotionally identical. Therefore, women and men are not entitled to the same rights and opportunities.

Once the equivocation is removed, it is clear that the argument's conclusion is neither supported by nor even related to the premise. No reason is offered to show that physical and emotional differences imply different rights and opportunities.

false cause: generic term for any questionable conclusion about cause and effect. To figure out specifically *why* the conclusion is (said to be) questionable, go back to Chapter V.

false dilemma: reducing the options you consider to just two, often diametrically opposed to each other and unfair to the people against whom the dilemma is posed. For example, "America: Love It or Leave It." A more subtle example from a student paper: "Since the universe could not have been created out of nothingness, it must have been created by an intelligent life force. . . ." Well, maybe, but is creation by an intelligent life force the *only* other possibility? This argument **overlooks alternatives.**

Ethical arguments seem especially prone to false dilemmas. Either the fetus is a human being with all the rights you and I have, we say, or else it is a lump of tissue with no moral significance at all. Either every use of animal products is wrong, or all of the current uses are acceptable. In fact, other possibilities usually exist. Try to increase the number of options you consider, not narrow them!

loaded language: language that primarily plays on the emotions. It does not make an argument at all, in truth, but is only a form of manipulation. See Rule 5.

non sequitur: drawing a conclusion that "does not follow," that is, a conclusion that is not a reasonable inference from, or even related to, the evidence. This is a very general term for a bad argument. Try to figure out specifically what is supposed to be wrong with it.

overgeneralizing: generalizing from too few examples. Just because your student friends are all athletes or business majors or vegetarians, it doesn't follow that *all* of your fellow students are the same (remember Rules 7 and 8). You can't even generalize from a large sample unless it is demonstrably representative. Take care!

overlooking alternatives: forgetting that things may happen for a variety of reasons, not just one. For example, Rule 19 pointed out that just because events E_1 and E_2 may correlate, it does not follow that E_1 causes E_2. E_2 could cause E_1; something else could cause *both* E_1 and E_2; E_1 may cause E_2 *and* E_2 may cause E_1; or E_1 and E_2 might not even be related. **False dilemma** is another example: there are usually many more options than two!

persuasive definition: defining a term in a way that may seem to be straightforward but in fact is loaded. For example, someone might define "Evolution" as "the atheistic view that species develop as a result of mere chance events over a supposed period of billions of years." Persuasive definitions may be favorably loaded too: for example, someone might define a "conservative" as "a person with a realistic view of human limits."

petitio principii: Latin for **begging the question**

poisoning the well: using **loaded language** to disparage an argument before even mentioning it

> I'm confident you haven't been taken in by those few holdouts who still haven't outgrown the superstition that . . .

More subtly:

> No sensitive person thinks that . . .

post hoc, ergo propter hoc (literally, "after this, therefore because of this"; sometimes just called the *post hoc fallacy*): assuming causation too readily on the basis of mere succession in time. Again a very general term for what Chapter V tries to make precise. Return to Chapter V and try to figure out if other causal explanations are more plausible.

red herring: introducing an irrelevant or secondary subject and thereby diverting attention from the main subject. Usually the red herring is an issue about which people get heated quickly, so that no one notices how their attention is being diverted. In a discussion of the relative safety of different makes of cars, for instance, the issue of which cars are made in America is a red herring.

straw man: a caricature of an opposing view, exaggerated from what anyone is likely to hold, so that it is easy to refute. See Rule 5.

Appendix II

Definitions

Some arguments require attention to the meaning of words. Sometimes we may not know the established meaning of a word, or the established meaning may be specialized. If the conclusion of your argument is that "Wejacks are herbivorous," your first task is to define your terms, unless you are speaking to an Algonquian ecologist.[12] If you encounter this conclusion elsewhere, the first thing you need is a dictionary.

Other times, a term may be in popular use but still unclear. We debate "assisted suicide," for example, but don't necessarily understand exactly what it means. Before we can argue effectively about it, we need an agreed-upon idea of what we are arguing *about*.

Still another kind of definition is required when the meaning of a term is contested. What is a "drug," for example? Is alcohol a drug? Is tobacco? What if they are? Can we find any logical way to answer these questions?

D1

When terms are unclear, get specific

A neighbor of mine was taken to task by the city's Historic Districts Commission for putting up a four-foot model lighthouse in her front yard. City ordinances prohibit any yard fixtures in historic districts. She was hauled before the commission and told to remove it. A furor erupted and the story got into the newspapers.

---

[12] "Wejack" is the Algonquian name for the fisher, a weasel-like animal of eastern North America. "Herbivores" are animals that eat only or mostly plants. Actually, wejacks are not herbivorous.

Here the dictionary saved the day. According to *Webster's,* a "fixture" is something fixed or attached, as to a building, such as a permanent appendage or structural part. The lighthouse, however, was moveable—more like a lawn ornament. Hence, it was not a "fixture"—seeing as the law did not specify any alternative definition. Hence, not prohibited.

When issues get more difficult, dictionaries are less helpful. Dictionary definitions often offer synonyms, for one thing, that may be just as unclear as the word you're trying to define. Dictionaries also may give multiple definitions, so you have to choose between them. And sometimes, dictionaries are just plain wrong. *Webster's* may be the hero of the last story, but it also defines "headache" as "a pain in the head"—far too broad a definition. A bee sting or cut on your forehead or nose would be a pain in the head but not a headache.

For some words, then, you need to make the term more precise yourself. Use concrete, definite terms rather than vague ones (Rule 4). Be specific without narrowing the term too much.

> Organic foods are foods produced without chemical fertilizers or pesticides.

Definitions like this call a clear idea to mind, something you can investigate or evaluate. Be sure, of course, to *stick* to your definition as you go on with your argument (no equivocation).

One virtue of the dictionary is that it is fairly neutral. *Webster's* defines "abortion," for example, as "the forcible expulsion of the mammalian fetus prematurely." This is an appropriately neutral definition. It is not up to the dictionary to decide if abortion is moral or immoral. Compare a common definition from one side of the abortion debate:

> "Abortion" means "murdering babies."

This definition is loaded. Fetuses are not the same as babies, and the term "murder" unfairly imputes evil intentions to well-intentioned people (however wrong the writer may think they are). That ending the life of a fetus is comparable to ending the life of a baby is an arguable proposition, but it is for an argument to *show*—not simply *assume* by definition. (See also Rule 5, and the fallacy of persuasive definition.)

You may need to do a little research. You will find, for example, that "assisted suicide" means allowing doctors to help aware and rational people arrange and carry out their own dying. It does not include allowing doctors to "unplug" patients without their consent (that would be some form of "involuntary euthanasia"—a different category). People may have good reasons to object to assisted suicide so defined, but if the definition is made clear at the outset, at least the contending parties will be talking about the same thing.

Sometimes we can define a term by specifying certain tests or procedures that determine whether or not it applies. This is called an *operational* definition. For example, Wisconsin law requires that all legislative meetings be open to the public. But what exactly counts as a "meeting" for purposes of this law? The law offers an elegant criterion:

> A "meeting" is any gathering of enough legislators to block action on the legislative measure that is the subject of the gathering.

This definition is far too narrow to define the ordinary word "meeting." But it does accomplish the purpose of this law: to prevent legislators from making crucial decisions out of the public eye.

When terms are contested, work from the clear cases

Sometimes a term is *contested.* That is, people argue over the proper application of the term itself. In that case, it's not enough simply to propose a clarification. A more involved kind of argument is needed.

When a term is contested, you can distinguish three relevant sets of things. One set includes those things to which the term clearly applies. The second includes those things to which the term clearly does *not* apply. In the middle will be those things whose status is unclear—including the things being argued over. Your job is to formulate a definition that

1. *includes* all the things that the term clearly fits;

2. *excludes* all the things that the term clearly does not fit; and

3. draws the *plainest possible line* somewhere in between, and *explains* why the line belongs there and not somewhere else.

For example, consider what defines a "bird." Exactly what is a bird, anyway? Is a bat a bird?

To meet requirement 1, it is often helpful to begin with the general category (*genus*) to which the things being defined belong. For birds, the natural genus would be animals. To meet requirements 2 and 3, we then need to specify how birds differ from other animals (the *differentia*). Our question therefore is: precisely what differentiates birds—*all* birds and *only* birds—from other animals?

It's trickier than it may seem. We can't draw the line at flight, for example, because ostriches and penguins don't fly (so the proposed definition wouldn't cover all birds, violating the first requirement), and bumblebees and mosquitoes do (so the proposed definition would include some nonbirds, violating the second).

What distinguishes all and only birds, it turns out, is having feathers. Penguins and ostriches have feathers even though they don't fly—they're still birds. But flying insects do not, and neither (in case you were wondering) do bats.

Now consider a harder case: what defines a "drug"?

Start again with the clear cases. Heroin, cocaine, and marijuana clearly are drugs. Air, water, most foods, and shampoos clearly are *not* drugs—though all of these are "substances," like drugs, and are all ingested or applied to our body parts. Unclear cases include tobacco and alcohol.[13]

Our question, then, is: Does any general description cover *all* of the clear cases of drugs and *none* of the substances that clearly aren't drugs, drawing a clear line in between?

A drug has been defined—even by a presidential commission—as a substance that affects mind or body in some way. But this definition is far too broad. It includes air, water, food, and so on, too, so it fails on the second requirement.

We also can't define a drug as an *illegal* substance that affects mind or body in some way. This definition might cover more or less the right set of substances, but it does not meet requirement 3. It does not explain why the line belongs where it is. After all, part of the point of trying to define "drug" in the first place might well be to decide which substances *should* be legal and which should not! Defining a drug as an illegal substance

---

[13] Unclear in another way are substances such as aspirin, antibiotics, vitamins, and antidepressants—the kinds of substances we buy in "drugstores" and call "drugs" in a pharmaceutical sense. But these are *medicines* and not drugs in the moral sense we are exploring.

short-circuits this project. (Technically, it commits the fallacy of begging the question.)

Try this:

> A "drug" is a substance used primarily to alter our state of mind in some specific way.

Heroin, cocaine, and marijuana obviously count. Food, air, and water don't —because even though they have effects on the mind, the effects are not specific and are not the primary reason why we eat, breathe, and drink. Unclear cases we then approach with the question: is the *primary* effect *specific* and on the *mind?* Perception-distorting and mood-altering effects do seem to be the chief concern in current moral debates about drugs, so arguably this definition captures the kind of distinction people really want to make.

Should we add that drugs are addictive? Maybe not. Some substances are addictive but not drugs—certain foods, perhaps. And what if a substance that "alter[s] our state of mind in some specific way" turns out to be *non*addictive (as some people have claimed about marijuana, for example)? Is it therefore not a drug? Maybe addiction defines "drug *abuse*," but not "drug" as such.

D3
Definitions don't replace arguments

Definitions help us to organize our thoughts, group like things with like, and pick out key similarities and differences. Sometimes, after words are clearly defined, people may even discover that they do not really disagree about an issue at all.

By themselves, though, definitions seldom settle difficult questions. We seek to define "drug," for example, partly to decide what sort of stance to take toward certain substances. But such a definition cannot answer this question by itself. Under the proposed definition, coffee is a drug. Caffeine certainly alters the state of the mind in specific ways. It is even addictive. But does it follow that coffee should be banned? No, because the effect is mild and socially positive for many people. Some attempt to weigh benefits against harms is necessary before we can draw any conclusions.

Marijuana is a drug under the proposed definition. Should *it* (continue to) be banned? Just as with coffee, more argument is necessary. Some people claim that marijuana has only mild and socially positive effects too. Supposing they're right, you could argue that marijuana shouldn't be banned even though it is a drug (like coffee). Others argue that it has far worse effects and tends to be a "gateway" to harder drugs besides. If they're right, you could argue for banning marijuana whether it is a drug or not.

Or perhaps marijuana is most akin to certain antidepressants and stimulants—medicines that (take note) also turn out to be drugs on the proposed definition, but call not for bans but for *control.*

Alcohol, meanwhile, is a drug under the proposed definition. In fact, it is the most widely used drug of all. Its harms are enormous, including kidney disease, birth defects, half of all traffic deaths, and more. Should it be limited or banned? Maybe—although there are counterarguments too. Once again, though, this question is not settled by the determination that alcohol is a drug. Here the *effects* make the difference.

In short, definitions contribute to clarity, but seldom do they make arguments all by themselves. Clarify your terms—know exactly what questions you're asking—but don't expect that clarity alone will answer them.

Resources

The general subject of this book is usually labeled "critical thinking." If you're a student wanting to learn more about the subject, look for Critical Thinking courses offered at your school. To read more, you can find dozens of textbooks for such courses online or in college or university libraries. One good recent example is Lewis Vaughn's *The Power of Critical Thinking,* 2nd ed. (New York: Oxford University Press, 2007).

Critical thinking used to be called "informal logic"—in contrast to the formal kind. The study of *formal* logic begins with the deductive forms presented in Chapter VI and expands them into a symbolic system of much greater scope. If you want to look in that direction, once again there are dozens of textbooks and other guides available, this time under the keywords "logic" or "symbolic logic." Some textbooks combine formal and informal logic: a fine example is David Kelley, *The Art of Reasoning,* 3rd ed. (New York: W. W. Norton, 1998).

The field of *rhetoric* examines the persuasive use of language, especially in arguments. One good text in the field is *The Aims of Argument: A Text and Reader,* 4th ed., by Timothy Crusius and Carolyn Channell (New York: McGraw-Hill, 2003). For an "invitational," non-combative approach to rhetoric and oral argumentation, see Sonja and Karen Foss, *Inviting Transformation: Presentational Speaking for a Changing World,* 2nd ed. (Long Grove, IL: Waveland Press, 2002). A useful guide to the rhetorical as well as logical "moves" in academic writing in particular is Gerald Graff and Cathy Birkenstein's *They Say, I Say* (New York: W. W. Norton, 2006).

On the role of critical thinking in ethics, see my book *A 21st Century Ethical Toolbox,* 2nd ed. (New York: Oxford University Press, 2008). On the role of ethics in critical thinking, see *The Ethical Practice of Critical Thinking* by Martin Fowler (Chapel Hill, NC: Carolina Academic Press, 2008).

On creativity, my little book *Creativity for Critical Thinkers* (New York: Oxford University Press, 2007) may be helpful. On the creative writing of arguments, see Frank Cioffi, *Imaginative Argument: A Practical Manifesto for Writers* (Princeton, NJ: Princeton University Press, 2005).

Specifically on the fallacies, see Howard Kahane and Nancy Cavendar, *Logic and Contemporary Rhetoric,* 10th ed. (Belmont, CA: Wadsworth, 2005).

On style, still unmatched is William Strunk and E. B. White's *The Elements of Style* (New York: Macmillan, many editions)—a book in spirit much like this one. Keep them together on a shelf somewhere, and don't let them gather dust!